In My Seat

A Pilot's Story from Sept 10th - 11th

Megan Ann Scheibner

Afterword by:

Dr. Steve Scheibner

Cover design: Dorian LaChance
Back Cover photo: Peter Scheibner

Printed in the United States of America
2012

Library of Congress Cataloging-in-Publication Data

ISBN-978-0-9849714-0-4

To Steve: Thanks for taking me along on this journey. You are my best friend and the love of my life!

And

To my kids: Kaitlyn, Peter, Emma, Molly, Nate, Baleigh, Stephen, Tate, and my "not a daughter" Emerson:
I may never finish the family scrapbooks, (there's a surprise) but now you'll always know our story. I love you all!

Contents

The sun beat warmly on Tom McGuinness' shoulders as he finished his pre-flight inspection of American Airlines Flight 11. His early morning duties were made more bearable by the beautiful, sunny New England morning. With the outside of the airplane inspected and prepared, Tom returned to the cockpit to complete the pre-flight brief with Captain John Ogonowski. The exterior walk-around and brief were as natural to Tom as breathing. He had practiced them so many times that they were second-nature, just a part of who he was as a First Officer for American Airlines.

Captain Ogonowski: "Tom, let's brief the takeoff. This will be your takeoff and landing today. We will be departing on runway 22R, using standard power. Our departure clearance is the Logan 6 departure. Don't start your turn-out to a heading of 140 until at least 400 feet. In the event of an emergency, such as: engine fire or failure on the runway, I plan to abort the takeoff. However, if we have a malfunction prior to rotate that will allow the airplane to fly safely, plan to continue the takeoff and we will handle the emergency airborne. The highest obstacle on our departure route is downtown Boston with an MSA of 2200 feet. Do you have any questions?"

First Officer Tom McGuinness: "If we have to return to the airport for any reason, I will plan to land on runway 22L. I'll fly the airplane and talk on the radios, while you run the emergency checklist. Any questions?"

While the cockpit crew was busy rehearsing their well-practiced take-off brief, another inhabitant of Flight 11 was busy rehearsing his own take-off scenario. Mohammed Atta slid into business class seat 8D. The connection from his Portland, Maine flight had been tighter than he would have liked and now he hurriedly settled into his seat to mentally prepare for the events that would soon follow. He had rehearsed his plan so many times; it was as much a part of who he was as the preflight was a part of Tom. He scanned the plane, making sure that his fellow conspirators were in their places. They were. Between First Class and Business Class, the soon-to-be hijackers filled five seats. All was going according to the plan.

Flight attendants Karen Martin and Barbara Arestegui completed their cabin preparations. They checked to make sure that everyone's seat belt was fastened and their tray tables were locked. They examined the seatbelt of Mohammed Atta; his safety was their main concern. Mohammed Atta examined the flight attendants as well, but he wasn't concerned for their safety; rather, he was concerned that they might try to stand in his way. To him they weren't humans, they were infidels, and as such, an obstruction to his well thought out plan. They would have to die.

Two states away, in Brunswick, Maine, Steve Scheibner stepped through the door to Wing Five, the headquarters of the Commodore of Naval Air Station Brunswick Maine. His unexpected day off from flying for American Airlines had provided an opportunity to meet with the Commodore to discuss a new pet project.

"Good morning, Sir!" barked the Command Duty Officer as Commander Scheibner stepped through the door. After 18 years in the Navy, the daily greeting and requisite salute were nothing new. He had practiced them so many times that they were ingrained into his being, just a part of who he was as a Naval Officer. Before stepping into the Commodore's office, Steve prayed a silent prayer for the man behind the door. For you see, that was just a part of Steve as well. As a Christian and the Pastor of a local church, the Commodore wasn't just his boss, he was a man that Steve cared for deeply and upheld in prayer. It didn't take much thought; praying was stamped into his heart and built into his life. It too, characterized who he was in every part of his life: Pastor, Commander, First Officer, husband and father.

Three men, all well-practiced at their chosen professions, all ready to do whatever was necessary to complete their day's mission, all intersected at one horrific moment in time that would change their lives forever...

7:40 a.m. Tom McGuinness dialed "Clearance Delivery" on frequency 121.65 to gain a push-back clearance.

7:43 a.m. Both engines on the Boeing 767 roared to life and Tom called ground control for taxi instructions.

8:00 a.m. American Airlines Flight 11 was cleared for takeoff by Boston Tower. Tom pushed the power levers forward and as the engines howled, passengers and crew alike were pushed back in their seats by the airplane's acceleration.

At 143 knots, Captain John Ogonowski called "rotate." Tom pulled back on the yoke and the flight to Los Angeles began.

The flight leveled at 26,000 feet and Tom engaged the autopilot.

8:13 a.m. Air Traffic Control instructed the crew to turn 20 degrees right. John replied, "American 11, turning 20 degrees right."

That would be the cockpit crew's last transmission... Removing his seat belt, Mohammed Atta rose from his seat. Tom's mission was over; Atta's would now begin.

For the next 32 minutes, Atta and his co-conspirators carried out their reign of terror. In that time, they would slash the throats of both John and Tom and stab the two flight attendants from First Class. They herded the passengers to the rear compartment of the airplane and contained them with mace and pepper spray. They admonished the passengers to cooperate and they would all live. They lied...

8:46 a.m. Gripping the yoke with blood stained hands and fueled with a fanatical frenzy, Mohammed Atta slammed the huge 767 into the North Tower of the World Trade Center. No one aboard Flight 11 would survive.

Three men...three missions. The horrific events of September 11th would end the mission of two; but one lived on... and that's where the story really begins...

Preface

This book began as a video—"In My Seat: A Pilot's Story"—which has quickly become an internet phenomenon. Or as my teenagers often say, "It's gone viral."

That's no exaggeration!

As of this writing, "In My Seat" has generated more than 1.6 million visits on YouTube [1]—along with a flood of e-mails, and it has thrust my family into the limelight in a way that we never expected.

When our story first hit the Web and literally began to explode in popularity, I found myself asking, "God, Why us?" I mean, what's so special about the Scheibner clan? Steve and I are down-to-earth people: We're busy raising our kids, serving in church, and carving out a living in our little corner of the world—just as millions of other Americans do every day from coast to coast. We cherish our kids and love our "safe haven" in rural Maine. So why have we been plucked out of the crowd? As I ponder that question and talk it over endlessly with the Lord, the same, gentle answer always comes back to me: "*Why not you?*"

You see, the impact that the video is having on tens of thousands of people and everything that I'm about to share in this book isn't really about Steve and our family—or even about the events of September 11, 2001. These pages tell the timeless story of our one, true God and what His Son, Jesus Christ, accomplished on the cross.

---

[1] To view "In My Seat" go to this link:
http://characterhealth.com/videos/InMySeat.html

No, Steve and I aren't anything special. (We're fairly ordinary people.) But the God we serve is *extraordinary*: "The Son is the radiance of God's glory and the exact representation of his being, sustaining all things by his powerful word" (Hebrews 1:3, NIV).

And as I look back over the last decade of our lives, I can see exactly how He has prepared the Scheibner household for the ministry that He has laid before us.

In 2002, Steve preached a sermon that contained these three points: (1) We must be eager participants in our own spiritual growth. (2) We must be willing to take radical risks. (3) We must be wholly submitted to the Word of God.

These three points summarize Steve's life and the way that he has approached his Christian walk. Because he is a man who has lived out what he preaches, God has been delighted to fill his spiritual lamp with oil. In fact, the Lord has ignited that oil into a bonfire of passion for God, which is sparking a flame in others, as well.

The answer to my "why-us" question is also this: God doesn't prepare people with His message just so that they can be a decorative lamp, set on a mantel, admired but never used. Steve's life, and our family's mission, has always been to be eager and available to serve God—wherever and whenever He calls us. This is yet another opportunity to obey His will. For years, our Heavenly Father has been preparing the whole Scheibner family for this time, and now it's our privilege to show God to a watching world. He has provided the story—and the audience. Now it is time for us to turn the spotlight on Him.

As you'll see, Steve's story is a "God story." Before Steve knew God, our Creator knew Steve. He was actively involved in preparing my husband for a ministry that Steve couldn't begin to fathom. *To God be the glory, great things He has done.*

Megan Ann Scheibner
November 2011

Introduction:
From September 10th to the 11th

I can't begin to count the number of times that God, in His mercy, has comforted and quieted me during life's trials and moments of fear. On September 10, 2001, He was beginning the process of reminding me of His presence, care, and control, long before I had any clue that I would be in need of those reminders.

September 10th was an extravagantly beautiful day in Maine. There is nothing more pleasant than a blue New England sky, and on that Monday the sky was crystal clear. After finishing their home schooling for the day, our oldest children spent time at a nursing home, visiting with elderly friends and running errands for the staff. I picked them up at about 1:00 p.m., and with baby in tow, we headed to the library.

The library, in our little town, is built to look like a small castle. It almost appears to have been plucked from the pages of one of my children's books, and it is one of our favorite destinations. I sent my children inside to search for books and to use the computers, while I lingered outside and enjoyed a cup of coffee in the library park gazebo. After two years spent moving and settling into a new routine in Maine, it felt good to just relax and to begin to enjoy our new normalcy. No more trips to New York City for Steve; now he would fly out of Boston. For me, no more worrying about the employee parking lot with its carjackers and the dangerous and aggressive drivers and traffic my husband faced with every trip to the airport.

Looking around the library park that peaceful afternoon, I saw the hand of God. He was there in the leaves and the sky and in the laughter of children coming and going from the library. That afternoon, another family, the McGuinness family, was seeing the hand of God, as well. As they celebrated Tom's 42nd birthday, everyone spent time sharing thanks for his leadership and his Christian testimony. The Lord was in their midst just as He was with my family on that beautiful September day. For us, God was alive.

At that very moment, however, another man was viewing the same beauty and seeing not the hand of God, but the blueprint of another. Mohammed Atta was surrounded by the very same God-breathed creation that Tom McGuinness and I could see, but he answered to another master. (Essentially, his God-vision had been blinded.) He didn't see our Creator in the leaves and in the sky. He didn't experience our Heavenly Father in a loving Christian family. Instead, he spent that beautiful day plotting destruction, darkness, and hatred. His plan was to exterminate God and God's people. What a contrast.

***

As I sat in the quiet gazebo, enjoying the clear skies and the multi-colored leaves, I prayed silently: "Thank you, God. Thank you that we are all here together. Thank you for meaningful work. Thank you for a safe place to raise our children. Thank you for peace, and normalcy, and routine." At that moment, life was so good. I had no idea what the next twenty-four hours held in store for our family, our country, and really, our world.

I finished my coffee and gathered the children to drive back home. When I got there, Steve told me that he was headed to Los Angeles the next day. That was no surprise. Because he needed Sundays off to pastor the new church plant, weekday trips had become the regular routine for his flying. We got his suitcase from the car, emptied out the old laundry, and began to prepare for his trip to the West Coast.

I ironed Steve's shirt and made sure that all of the parts of his uniform were ready. Steve packed his airline kit bag and double-checked that he had all of the necessary maps and publications. He loaded the car and we settled in to spend the evening doing family stuff with the kids. Strangely, however, he never received a phone call from American Airlines confirming that the trip assigned to him via the computer had been finalized and locked in as his trip.

The Sleep of the Unaware

The "no phone call" wasn't completely unheard of for our family. In Steve's time at American Airlines, there had been about three times that we prepared for him to leave and the phone never rang. Sometimes we wishfully joked, "Perhaps you'll get bumped from your trip and be able to hang out with us today." But usually, that just didn't happen. For us, no phone call meant more time with Dad and he would still get paid, not a bad deal.

So that evening, back into the closet went the airline uniform and instead, we prepared Steve's Navy uniform. The unexpected day off from the airlines provided an opportunity to spend time working on the Navy base. Again, I ironed another uniform and made sure his insignia were in place. Now, with a plan in place for Tuesday the 11th, we tucked the kids in bed and headed upstairs ourselves.

Forty-five minutes away, Mohammed Atta spent the evening in a rented hotel room. No family dinner for him. Instead, he went to the local Pizza Hut and then returned to his room, eager to perform his prescribed rituals in anticipation of the next day's events. While we slept in Georgetown, Maine, Mohammed Atta stayed awake, fueling his hatred and evil plans, in Portland, Maine. In a hotel that we passed on each trip to the "big city" of Portland, Steve's would-be assassin made his final preparations and yet, we slept peacefully.

I can only speculate about what was going on in the McGuinness household that evening. Their lives looked so much like ours on paper: military background, airline pilot, active in their church. I picture them going through the same pre-trip rituals that Steve and I performed. I'm sure Tom was in bed early; he would have to be at Logan early on Tuesday morning to preflight the airplane for Flight 11 to Los Angeles. Like us, they would sleep the sleep of the unaware.

Unaware that Monday night would be their final family night together.

Unaware that Tom's 42nd birthday would be his last.

Unaware that life, as they knew it, was about to change—*forever.*

Stunned Disbelief

Tuesday, September 11th was yet another beautiful day. We awakened to blue, cloudless skies and unseasonably warm temperatures, a good day to speed through our schoolwork and head outside; a good day to continue building that new family normalcy.

Steve dressed in his uniform and left early for the Navy base. He, too, wanted to get through his work and then come home to spend the afternoon with us. Shortly after Steve left, a crew of contractors showed up to finish some of the work still remaining on our new home. After months in and out of our house, the contractors had become our friends. They and the children often chatted and joked with each other.

By 9:00 a.m., we were well into our school day. Oddly, I began to notice the contractors walking behind me and whispering to one another. *Strange behavior,* I thought, but before I could find out what was wrong, my phone rang. It was the owner of the building company. He asked me where Steve was, which, at the time, seemed like a strange question. When I answered that he had gone to the Naval Air Station in Brunswick that morning, Tim asked me if I knew what was happening. He told me about the first airplane and as we were talking, the second plane hit the second tower.

Like the rest of the country, I was shocked and disbelieving. What was going on? I remember my knees felt weak, and I was breathless. Just then, call waiting beeped and Steve was on the line. I tearfully answered and Steve just kept saying, "Don't worry, it wasn't me … it wasn't me." In my head, I knew that he was safe, but at that same moment I had a horrifying thought shoot through my mind. I realized that at the same time that Steve was reassuring me, there would be another wife who was hearing the words, "I'm sorry, it was him, it was him." The thought was overwhelming, too big to comprehend. I stuffed it far back into my mind.

At that moment, I began to understand what was going on with the contractors. They were petrified that Steve had been on the flight … and they thought they'd have to take care of me. What in the world would they do with a distraught new widow? I reassured them that Steve was safe, turned on the TV, and we all huddled around the screen—staring in stunned disbelief.

For Steve, it was the beginning of an emotional rollercoaster. His phone began to ring off the hook even before he had a chance to call me. Friend after friend dialed his number, often sobbing on the other end of the line—thankful to hear his voice and to know that he was safe. Suddenly, the gravity of the situation began to hit home. The planes that went down were ones that Steve had flown. The pilots and crewmembers whose lives were taken in an unthinkable moment were more than coworkers; they were Steve's friends. Like everyone else during that horrible day, he just wanted to get home to me and to our children, but that was impossible. The Navy base had been locked down and no one was able to leave. Hours would pass before he could rejoin our family.

At home, members of the church began to call or stop by. Many were terrified by the prospect that their pastor had been one of the pilots on the Boston flight. Over and over, I assured them that he was fine. At one point, two deacons burst through the front door anxious to know that Steve was safe. The day was quickly becoming one tearful, emotional conversation after another. Steve called from the Navy base and encouraged me to invite all of the church members over that evening for an impromptu prayer meeting. Even in the midst of the chaos of his day, he recognized his responsibility to pastor the church and to help them process the day's events.

Our older children were glued to the TV and had so many questions. But for the younger children, the needs of the day continued. There were diapers to be changed, meals to be made, naps to be provided—all the normal parts of life with children. I couldn't escape the realization that other wives, just like me, were dealing with those same normal needs, all the while facing the reality that their husbands had been on those planes. I was so thankful for the distraction of caring for the children to keep those distressing thoughts at bay.

When Steve finally managed to leave the base and return home, it was impossible to do anything but cry and hold onto him. Even then, we didn't realize just how close we had come to never holding each other again.

Before the rest of the church arrived, Steve decided to try to find out who had been flying the trip. He logged into the American Airlines employee site and that's when the fullness of the providence of God became so clear.

When Steve pulled up the flight information from that day, he realized that the screen was the same one that he had seen the day before. On September 10th, Flight 11 had his name penciled in. Now his name was missing. Instead, these ominous words were typed in the spot that had held his name: *Sequence Failed Continuity*. For aviation professionals those three words mean one thing: the plane never made it to its destination.

I'll never forget the sound of Steve's voice as he called out my name later that afternoon. It was hoarse and gravelly ... and filled with stunned disbelief. When I spun around the corner and stopped in his office, he was sitting with his head bowed. The color had left his face. Steve pointed at his computer screen and said, "That's the trip I packed for. I should have been on that flight." He held me tightly—his entire body trembling.

I locked up inside.

All those emotions that I had been holding at bay all day now became a confused mass. I was thankful and relieved that Steve was safe, yet I felt sorrow—even guilt—for all the other wives and families. I simply did not know what to do with my conflicting feelings, so I just shut down emotionally. All through the prayer meeting that night, I couldn't share what was going on inside. I didn't cry. I just stared and went through the motions.

For me, the tears would come later after a phone call from the airline. In anticipation of flight operations resuming, Steve received a call from crew-scheduling at American Airlines, the very folks we expected to hear from the day before. This time, they were calling to confirm a trip assignment for the next day, Sept. 12th. Of all the trips that they could have assigned to Steve, they now wanted to assign him the same trip that was hi-jacked just hours earlier. The trip he narrowly missed on the 11th was now his on the 12th... AA flight 11!

I lost it.

I couldn't imagine saying goodbye to Steve and watching him drive away. Thankfully, God intervened and all of the scheduled flights were cancelled for the next four days.

Never the Same

The events of September 11th changed my husband. Steve had been faithfully serving God before the hijackings and he continued to serve Him at the church afterward, yet he was different.

He wasn't satisfied with the status quo anymore. Before, he had planned to stay at the church for the rest of his life. He called it his "Life's-work," and joked about being buried in the permafrost behind the church. Now, day-by-day, God began to redirect his life and the path our family would travel.

The unthinkable events onboard Flight 11 that morning played out on the intersection of several crossroads. When Mohammed Atta slashed Tom McGuinness' throat and threw his body into the first class compartment, Tom, because of his relationship with Jesus Christ, went to be with the Lord. For him, it was graduation day and the next step in his eternal walk with God.

For Mohammed Atta, when the airplane crashed into the first tower, nothing was what he expected. The false master who ruled his life had promised riches and reward. Instead, at that horrible moment, Atta realized the truth: He had been deceived. The same master would now mock him for eternity. He had been nothing more than a puppet in Satan's futile plan to eradicate God; a foolish and expendable puppet.

Atta thought he killed God that day. He was wrong. Instead, a spark was lit in one of God's men that would begin to burn and to grow until it became a consuming flame. God used the events of September 11th to change Steve Scheibner from a man contentedly doing His will as a church planter in a small town in Maine, into a man consumed by the urgency of reaching a nation for Christ. God used the days following September 11th to hone and to continue to prepare Steve for the ministry the Lord had in mind. God showed Steve what it meant to live like a "borrowed-time believer;" one who realized that every day, every moment, every breath, was a gift from God. The Lord used a smoking hole on national TV to light a fire in Steve's heart that would change the direction of Steve's life for good.

Tom McGuinness filled a seat that should have been Steve's. He died a horrific death that should have been my husband's, as well. But he didn't die for Steve's sins. Jesus Christ paid that price for him and for Tom. And as each day passed after the hijackings, that truth became more vivid for Steve. At first, he was hesitant to share his story, but with each passing year, God made it clear that this was His message and that Steve was simply the messenger to paint a picture for a lost and dying world.

Romans 8:28 tells us that God works all things together for His good. In the years following September 11th, God has begun to show us what that good looks like. No longer is the story about one pilot dying for another. Instead, God's story is shining through. Tom's death, in Steve's seat, has provided a clear, modern-day picture of substitutionary atonement. People get it. Tom's death was not in vain. God has used it to show people what it means to have another die in their place. Jesus Christ is exalted as people recognize the substitutionary price He paid for them. The seat He filled for them. What Mohammed Atta meant for evil, God is using for good.

***

D.L. Moody once said, "The world has yet to see what God can do with and for and through and in and by the man who is fully and wholly consecrated to Him." September 11, 2001, was the match that lit the fuse in one such man, and now that fuse has become a blazing fire.

I know that man.

I'm proud to say that Steve Scheibner is my husband and my best friend … and that he is a man determined to live each day urgently and steadfastly to the glory of God. He is a man fully and wholly consecrated to God.

This is his story.

Chapter 1

Never Say "Can't"

The story of Steve's life is really the story of God, through circumstances and people, putting oil in one man's lamp. Although at times, Steve would have seemed like an unlikely choice for God's "oil filling" program, ultimately, his willingness to be changed and conformed to the image of Christ prepared him to be a vessel suitable for the Master's work.

Steve was born on October 21, 1960. Before we were even married, I remember his mother telling me how she almost didn't make it to the labor room. Steve was so anxious to be born that the hospital orderly had to pick up my mother-in-law, a tiny woman, and run for the operating room. She told me this story in conjunction with letting me know that Stephen, as she called him, was always in a hurry and had been ready to be married since the time he was in Kindergarten; I was just the one who finally said yes. Not exactly reassuring. In fact, however, she was absolutely right. Steve, himself, told me of his first love: a girl named Debbie Sprinkle. She, to his discerning Kindergartner eyes, was just about perfect, with long hair and a charming smile. I guess I'm just lucky she never realized how he felt about her!

Just a side note about Steve and the fact that his mother called him Stephen. Before Steve was born, his mother picked out different names for her soon-to-be-born child, according to the dates on the calendar. If Steve had been born on October 20th, his name would have been Christian. An appropriate name, I suppose. However, if Steve had been born on October

22nd, his name would have been Rocky! *Rocky?* Are you kidding me? I'm just really thankful he picked the 21st to make his appearance. Although, as he always points out, about half of the 50-year old men in the United States are named Steve and he's convinced it's because their mothers had crushes on Steve McQueen. To his mom, he would always be Stephen, not Steve, and when she was upset with him, that name could stretch to at least six syllables.

By the time Steve was born, his family was already in turmoil. Steve's father, Warren, was a gifted piano player, making his living playing for dances and clubs. At the same time, he was also a serious alcoholic. Steve's mom, Marion, a conscientious clerk for the Michigan Central Railroad, was already beginning to tire of Warren's unpredictability and irresponsibility. By the time that Steve was two, Warren's drinking had escalated to the point that Marion was compelled ask him to leave, and she became the single mother of her son and two daughters, Susan and Linda.

According to Steve's mother, her boy was "the perfect child." She remembers him asking to go to bed at night and never ever causing any trouble. Although I can believe the bedtime part—he still disappears at night, sometimes, and I find him fast asleep—his sisters strongly disagree with the "never causing trouble" part. Once, when Steve was three, his mother went out to get the mail. He watched her walk to the mailbox, then back to the front door and just as she reached for the handle, he locked it! Then, he bolted for the back door to lock her out there, as well. She was just lucky that she could run faster than his short toddler legs could propel him. Another time, he and his sister, Linda, argued so vehemently over who should get the last Twinkie that his mother went to the grocery story, bought all of the available Twinkies, and made the two of them eat every one of the pastries. Perfect child? Never caused trouble? I'm not so sure…

Street Smarts (and a *Smart* Mouth)

Although his marriage was over, Warren remained an integral part of his son's life. He would take Steve to visit his half-brothers, Warren's sons from his first marriage, and he often kept Steve at his apartment for the weekend. As well, he picked up Steve from school every day at lunchtime and took him bowling. That's right—bowling. At one point, Steve thought that he would grow up to be a professional bowler. In fact, one of his worst memories from childhood was his first bowling awards banquet. He received an "I tried" trophy, which to his six-year old mind was a total insult. Steve realized that his team had come in last place and a trophy with the inscription, "I Tried," irked his young principled mind to no end. He was so offended and determined to get the winner's trophy from that time on. Once he moved away from Michigan and his dad's daily bowling dates, the dream to be a professional bowler disappeared. Honestly, I can't say I'm sorry about that change in direction!

I grew up in rural Pennsylvania, and when I first met Steve, I used to marvel at how confident and unafraid he seemed to be when we went into Philadelphia for special dates. That confidence, really street smarts, came from his early years in Detroit. Where I had memories of playing kickball outside our house, Steve's memories involved waiting for his dad to get home from piano gigs and hiding because he heard gunfire in the street below his dad's apartment. Living in downtown Detroit taught Steve to protect himself and to always have one eye open. Very reassuring to a nervous country kid, like me, but hardly the background you would picture for the man that Steve has become.

As a young boy, Steve had two strikes against him on the streets of Detroit. First, he wasn't very big. Just like all of our sons, Steve was small for his age and terribly skinny. Strike number two was this: Steve had, and continues to have, a very quick tongue, which got him in a lot of trouble. Because he was small, slow, and had a big mouth, he was in some sort of fight every day, until he finally left Detroit.

Although neither of Steve's parents were Christians, when he was very young, Steve's father did take him to church on occasion. His memories of those Sundays consist of arriving after the first hymn and leaving during the closing one. That was it, in and out, with no chance to be asked any questions or meet any church members. For Steve's father, it was like punching a "spiritual time clock." Technically, he went to church, but his heart wasn't in it. For Steve, it was just another chance to spend time with his dad.

And speaking of that, his father instilled in Steve a love for baseball. I love baseball, too, so we are the perfect pair, and ever since moving to New England, we have been happily sucked into the Red Sox Nation vortex. Once, when Steve was about seven years old, Warren took him to see the Detroit Tigers play a home game. In those days, if you weren't in your seat at the start of the inning, you stood patiently waiting for the inning to be over, so that you wouldn't disturb any other fans. As Steve and his dad stood waiting to be seated, a foul ball caromed off the metal rail in front of Steve, whacked him in the head, and knocked him out. When Steve came to, he was in the medical center with a giant knot on his head and NO

BASEBALL! In the hubbub of the accident, someone else had grabbed HIS baseball.

The Tigers players heard what had happened and graciously prepared a special gift. They passed a ball around the dugout and signed their autographs for the injured boy. That was special, but it gets even better. This was 1968. The Detroit team had players like Al Kaline, (a Hall of Famer) Denny McClain (the last pitcher to win 30 games in one season,) and Mickey Lolich. This was the team that would later come back from a three-game deficit to win the World Series that year. Little Stevie Scheibner had their autographs!

Now for the bad news: When Steve returned home from the baseball game, his mother took one look at the autographed baseball and told him, "put it away and keep it clean, it might be worth something someday." Well, Warren had a different plan for that ball. Almost immediately, he took Steve outside and began to throw the ball for him to catch. "Baseballs are meant to be played with!" he emphatically told his ex-wife. Soon, the autographs were smeared and the baseball was worn out. What was once a one-of-a-kind collector's dream had become nothing more than a playground toy. I'm not sure how that episode fit into God's training program for Steve, maybe He knew it wouldn't be good for us to get rich too quickly!

Working Toward a Major-League Future

As long as I have known Steve, he has been an incredibly hard worker. Both of us used to joke about starting a new self-help group and calling it Overachievers Anonymous. For me, the drive to overachieve just seems to be part of my personality, but for Steve, I think his inner drive came from encounters with people who told him, "You just can't," and "You're not smart enough," ... "You just don't have the right connections and talent." Steve took those kinds of comments to heart, and he has spent most of his life pushing himself to prove the naysayers wrong.

His first encounter with the "You Cant's" of life came in fourth grade. His teacher, Mrs. McWilliams—someone who should have retired years before she had Steve in her class—was famous for her three rulers she'd taped together. Mrs. McWilliams used this weapon to enforce the rules in her classroom. If a student had his fingers over the edge of the desk, *WHACK!* If your leg was beyond your seat, *WHACK!* She ruled with an iron fist, and no one was safe from her dreaded weapon.

One day, in late fall, Steve fell victim to Mrs. McWilliams. It was the first snowfall of the year and he began to stare out the window, daydreaming of the moment that the bell would ring and he would be free from his school-desk prison. As his eyes took in the outside world, he turned in his seat without realizing that his leg was extending into the aisle. His teacher snuck stealthily up behind him and *WHACK!* Then, she leaned in close to his ear and hissed, "Stevie Scheibner, you'll never make a living staring out the window!"

Several years ago, Steve was flying a trip from Los Angeles to Boston. As he stared out over the farmland of Kansas, the memory of Mrs. McWilliam's insult shot through his mind. Here he was, a pilot for a major airline, well paid to simply stare out the window. He suddenly realized that his teacher was wrong! For Steve, "You can't" had become "I will!"

I wish that was the end of the story with Mrs. McWilliams, but it isn't.

In her class and all through fourth grade, Steve's grades had been mediocre, and he had begun to believe that he wasn't ever going to be a good student. The next year, however, in fifth grade, he had his first male teacher, a teacher who loved kids and loved to teach. Steve flourished in this new environment! At the end of the first recording period, Steve received his report card and for the first time in his life, he had earned straight A's. He was so excited! As he came bounding out the classroom door, eager to rush home to show his mother, he ran straight into Mrs. McWilliams. She grabbed the report card out of his hands, looked down at him and said, "Are you as dumb as ever, Stevie Scheibner?" Then she glanced at the document, and without uttering another word, she flung it down the hall. As Steve scurried after it, he knew that he had won a personal victory. Just because Mrs. McWilliams had relegated him to the failure list didn't mean that failure had to be his reality.

Stern Hands of Protection

At the age of eight, Steve moved away from Livonia, Michigan, where he had been living with his mother and they relocated to Lincoln Park, Michigan. The reason for the move was a new stepfather. While working at the railroad, Marion had met and fallen in love with a new man. She married George Weber in 1968. While Warren had been a serious drunk, George was an even worse and angrier drinker. Normal life for Steve became a regular routine of George going on benders, getting angry, and finally, throwing Marion and Steve out of the house; only to get sober, feel sorry, and bring them home, again. Steve's Aunt Pauline and Uncle Russell became a refuge during these times. Childless themselves, they came to view Steve as a son and often included him on vacations. Their home became a place of stability for both Steve and his mother.

When George wasn't drinking, he shared stories with Steve about his time in the Army, during World War II. George described in detail his horrible memories of the storming of Omaha Beach and the terrible loss of life he witnessed. Despite George's terrible drinking and angry outbursts, young Steve developed a heart of pity for his stepfather and for the painful times he had experienced. As well, Steve developed the utmost respect for the military and in particular, the Navy; a respect that would later translate into a twenty-eight-year career.

Although the years of turmoil with George and Marion were difficult for Steve, God was watching over him, nonetheless. One family, in particular, took an interest in Steve, and their interest in and influence on him started Steve down the road that would ultimately lead him to Christ. While living in Lincoln Park, a neighborhood boy named Jimmy McKeckney became Steve's best friend. Steve spent a great deal of time with the McKeckney family and a few of his escapades with Jimmy are worth noting.

One day, Steve and Jimmy found some half-smoked cigarettes behind the McKeckney house. Without lighting them, the two boys began to pretend to smoke the cigarettes. Suddenly, and much to their dismay, Mr. McKeckney arrived on the scene. Sending his own son inside to await his terrible fate, the dad grabbed Steve by the back of his collar, pulled him to his tiptoes, and marched him down the block to his own front porch. During the entire painfully long walk, Mr. McKeckney lectured young Steve about the evils of tobacco and threatened to tell his mother what her only son had been doing. To this day, Steve has never so much as touched a cigarette and he's convinced it's because he received the "wrath of Mr. McKeckney" that day. Don't you wish there were more Mr. McKeckneys in the world? Today's parents are so afraid of offending others, that to intervene in the life of someone else's child is almost unheard of and rarely applauded. I, for one, am thankful for the lesson that concerned father had taught. Growing up in a house full of smokers, it's probable that without his influence, Steve would have had just one more bad habit to overcome during his life.

Another episode at the McKeckney's clearly shows God's protection over Steve's life, long before Steve was ready to recognize the hand of God. Behind the McKeckney's house was a tall apple tree with low branches, perfect for two little boys to climb up and hide amongst the leaves. One day, while Steve and Jimmy were playing in the tree, Steve climbed higher than he should have and plummeted from the tree. The fall itself would have been bad enough, but Steve landed on a pile of bricks stacked in the yard. Somehow, Steve managed to stagger home, where his mother took one look at him and sent him to bed. Fortunately, Steve's older sister, Linda, came in to check on him and noticed that his skin was grey, his eyes were black, and his breathing seemed funny.

Frightened, Linda insisted that her mother take him to the hospital. Once there, they discovered that Steve had fractured his skull and his brain was swelling. Steve was in rough shape, but God had it all under control. Providentially, a world-renowned brain surgeon, Dr. Gass, "just happened" to be in Detroit and at the very hospital where Steve had been admitted. He performed emergency brain surgery and saved Steve's life. Without Linda's insistence and Dr. Gass' expertise, that fall from the apple tree could have been the end of the story, but God had other plans for Steve.

Interestingly, although the only outward reminder of Steve's fall is a long indented scar down the side of his head, that accident turned out to be an unexpected blessing when Steve was going through the Navy's Aviation Officer Candidate School, many years later. Because little is known about brain injuries and the impact of climbing and descending to altitude, each afternoon Steve would report to the Medical Center where he would be hooked up to machines and told to take a nap for an hour. So, while all of his buddies were running and doing push-ups, sit-ups, and jumping jacks, their friend Steve was fast asleep, enjoying some R&R. I'm not sure how happy his friends would have been for him if they'd known where he was, but Steve certainly relished the extra rest!

Simple Acts of Love

Finally, and most importantly, the McKeckneys picked up Steve and took him to church and Sunday School. It was there that he began to hear the stories from the Bible and he began to develop a picture of what Jesus had done for him on the cross. Although he didn't trust Christ as his Savior just then, the foundation was beginning to be laid and a few drops of oil were stored in his lamp. For the McKeckneys, it was probably no big deal to include Steve with their family, but for Steve, it was a picture of an intact family with an aware and involved father.

Unbeknownst to Steve, big changes would come again the year he turned thirteen. During the time that George, his stepfather, was in the Army, he had been shot through the lung. Although he survived his injury, when Steve was in middle school, George developed cancer at the old injury site and quickly succumbed to his illness. The man in the home was gone again, but this time, it was just Steve and his mom. Linda was married with two children, and Susan was off on her own. Although he grieved for his stepfather, the newfound peace in their home was a relief to both Steve and Marion.

Just about this time, Steve's Aunt Pauline and Uncle Russell relocated with the railroad, to Pennsylvania. Steve's mom, Marion, and her sister

Pauline were more than just siblings. They were, and continued to be, until Marion's death, best friends. For years, they had gone to work together at the railroad and finished their evenings by calling one another to say goodnight. Because of this close relationship, and because she was concerned about the street gangs that Steve was beginning to associate with, Marion took the plunge and moved to Pennsylvania, as well. She was able to keep her job at the railroad and simply transferred from Michigan Central to Penn Central, a job she would keep and enjoy until her retirement, in 1986.

What a change for Steve. He and Marion moved into a brand new condominium in Chadds-Ford, Pennsylvania. Although this is now a busy suburb of Philadelphia, in 1974, it was a sleepy rural area populated by wealthy families who worked for A.I. Dupont and who lived among the horse and mushroom farmers. Although the pressure of the daily fights in Detroit was gone, moving from city boy to country boy presented Steve with some unique challenges. As well, he no longer had the privilege of time with his father, who by this time had gone through rehabilitation and was a recovering alcoholic. All of his old paradigms were changing.

This move was a chance for Steve and his mom to begin a new chapter in their lives. Marion quickly threw herself into condominium living, meeting new friends and joining new clubs. For Steve, it was time to start a new chapter as the new kid in a new high school. Although it was intimidating, it was in this new environment and with new friends, that Steve would begin to develop into the man he is today, but that is a story for the next chapter.

Chapter 2

In God's Perfect Timing

It was 1975, and Steve was about to begin his freshman year at Unionville High School in Kennett Square, Pennsylvania. Although he'd given up his dream of becoming a professional bowler, the Steve that entered high school that year hadn't really embraced the idea of academics and a path that led to college. To him, school was just a necessary evil. He loved woodworking, something he'd learned in his middle school shop classes, and just figured that he would be a furniture builder. Now, to his credit, he does beautiful work with wood and many of our pieces of furniture were designed and built by him. However, the predictable life of a cabinetmaker wasn't what God had in mind for Steve. Yes, Steve would be a builder of sorts, but not a maker of furniture. He had no idea then the ministries that he would help build in the future. Although he didn't yet have a relationship with Christ, God began to orchestrate Steve's friendships and interests to lead him down a different path.

On the first day of school, Steve boarded the bus for what would become his daily 45-minute commute. He dreaded the ordeal, yet with a working mom, he had no other choice. Each miserable ride felt like reenactments of the street fights in Detroit: testosterone-laden boys would invariably challenge each other to prove who was Unionville's toughest, mouthiest … crudest.

When Steve arrived home every afternoon, he was the classic picture of a latchkey kid. He made himself a snack and spent the afternoon watching cartoons. I was a bookworm and never watched a cartoon until I married Steve. It took me a long time to differentiate between Daffy Duck and Tweety Bird, but after many years I have become almost as cartoon literate as Steve. Being a latchkey kid in a new state was a lonely time for Steve, but that was about to soon change.

Finding Acceptance

In 1975, Steve made two important discoveries. First, he discovered and became a beloved part of the Shaner family. Pete and Alane Shaner, along with their mother, Charlotte, lived in the same condominium complex with Steve and his mother. When the three teenagers met at the bus stop, a forever friendship was born. Although Pete and Steve would have called themselves "best friends," at any one time, it was Steve and Pete versus Alane, or Alane and Steve versus Pete, or Pete and Alane versus Steve … you get the picture.

The Shaner home was a place of words. This was new and fascinating to Steve and he longed to spend every moment with these new friends. Mrs. Shaner was a greeting card writer, and she could turn any conversation into a pun-war or rhyming match. In the limited time I was able to spend with her before her death, Charlotte Shaner did more to encourage my writing than any other person in my adult life. She loved words and their usage and wanted others to experience the joy of language as well. Also, because she and her children spoke fluent German, Steve soon began to use German idioms and expressions as part of his normal vocabulary.

The Shaners were poor, but their home was filled with laughter. Nothing delighted them as much as "rendering someone odious"—a phrase that simply meant laughing at someone else's foolishness until no one could sit up any longer. Because they were equal opportunity "renderers," everyone had their turn at being the brunt of the good-natured humor, and no one felt singled out. Remember, Steve came from a home filled with angry alcoholics, so this type of fun and family unity was like nothing he'd every known and he was drawn to it like a moth is drawn to a flame. Spending time with the Shaners caused his vocabulary, speech, and self-confidence to grow. He could be himself, and although sometimes this meant being "rendered odious," he knew that he was loved and accepted.

Alane and Pete had definite plans for their future. Alane was a diligent student and Pete was doing all of the necessary work to gain an appointment to the Naval Academy. As Steve spent more time with the Shaners, he began to get more serious about academics, and he began to think about continuing his education after high school. Their influence on him was profound.

Building Dreams

The second major discovery that Steve made that year was this: He could act! Steve tried out for and quickly won parts in the school plays. Soon he was getting bigger and better roles, until finally, he was acting the lead in most of the school productions. He developed strong friendships with the other drama students. These kids weren't like the street kids he knew in Detroit. They had dreams and ambitions, and they encouraged Steve to embrace his potential as well. Soon, he was enrolled in college preparatory classes and taking the courses he would need to get accepted into college.

Steve found his voice on the stage. As the character George Gibbs in Thornton Wilder's "Our Town," he entered and won numerous competitions. He had found his niche and he loved it! His success on the stage gave him the confidence to try other things he would never have thought to attempt. A friend convinced him to try out for the position of bass drummer in the marching band. Steve had never played the drums in his life, but the next football game, there he was … marching and banging away on the bass drum. I'm constantly amazed at the things that Steve will attempt and in our 27 years of marriage, he's taught me to loosen up and risk looking a little foolish by trying new things. I must admit, life is much more fun his way; it just takes me longer to get there!

His new position as the lead actor in the school plays gained Steve recognition, which boosted his confidence. The "new kid" had become one of the leaders of his class. A memory he'll never forget involves our last name. When I married Steve, I went from a fairly simple last name, Pierce, to the often mispronounced, Scheibner. Our last name is pronounced *Shyb-ner*—a name that seems easy to us, but that is noticeably difficult for the rest of the world. High School was no exception, and Steve spent four years patiently correcting teachers and faculty for the mispronunciation of his last name.

Graduation came in the spring of 1978, and to no one's surprise, the principal called "Stephen Schreibner" to the stage. By now, the whole student body was aware of the name problem, so they promptly yelled, "Not Schreibner, SCHEIBNER!" Funny memory, but, that's not the end of the story. A full twenty-four years later, and one year after the events of September 11, 2001, Steve was invited back to address the student body at Unionville High School. As he was announced that day, the emcee introduced Mr. Stephen (you guessed it) Schreibner. From the back of the auditorium, Steve heard six voices yell, "Not Schreibner, SCHEIBNER!"

Six teachers still remained from his days at Unionville, and they still remembered that troublesome last name!

A Drive for Independence

As soon as Steve turned 16, he received his driver's license. From that day on, he was finished with the school bus forever. Our children are home schooled and never rode the bus a single day of their lives, yet he still regales them with stories about the "lawless zone" that is the school bus. With a trust fund provided by his grandmother, Steve bought his first car. He has always loved cars and his first one was no exception. He picked up a 1968 black Ford Mustang with a 289 V8. *Wow!* He loved that muscle machine, and as it has been with his subsequent cars, he landed a great deal. Steve paid only $850.00 for the Mustang, which had only 35,000 miles on it. (His heart was broken when it was stolen many years later.)

The new car brought new freedom and he was no longer stuck at home as a latchkey kid. Steve got his first job working at the local Ramada Inn as a busboy. His experience working there was what helped him to secure his next, much more prestigious job at the renowned Dilworthtown Inn. Steve still remembers that job as one of his most demanding. It was there that he learned important lessons about excellence and attention to detail. These lessons still show up in the decisions that Steve makes about our family and our ministry. His goal is this: Give every task your best effort so that others might see the excellence of Christ. "Whatever you do, work at it with all your heart, as working for the Lord, not for men, since you know that you will receive an inheritance from the Lord as a reward" (Colossians 3:23-24).

That standard of excellence even showed up in the pranks that Steve initiated during his years at Unionville High School. I would love to share them with you, but I've been placed under a gag order and the consequences for disobeying it would be severe! Besides, we're not sure that the statute of limitations has run out on his crimes. However, it has been widely rumored that Steve may, or may not, have had something to do with a midnight prank that involved turning all of the books backwards (paper edge out) in the school library. Clearly, young Steve had too much free time and too little supervision!

Steve's interaction with the Shaners was a catalyst in his decision to study German and eventually take a trip as an exchange student to that country. In the summer after his junior year of high school, he boarded an airplane and left to spend the summer in Diepholz, Germany. This experience of living overseas and communicating with all types of different people would stand him in good stead when many years later, he became a pastor in northern New England.

Shortly after returning from his student exchange, Steve met a man who would influence him deeply and be instrumental in changing the direction of his life. When Steve entered Unionville High School in the fall of his senior year, he noticed someone that seemed to be out of place. Standing in the lobby was this old guy—he was all of 25 years old—complete with a full moustache, (remember the 70's?) and talking to some of his friends. Driven by curiosity, Steve wandered over to meet the stranger. He soon learned that the guy's name was Scott Hamilton and he was just at the high school to get to know the kids and spend time with them.

My Steve is a pretty cynical guy and that explanation just didn't seem right to him. In reality, Scott was the new area director for Young Life, an outreach ministry to high school kids, and he was doing exactly what Young Life had trained him to do. The organization believed then and still believes today that by building relationships with kids, older Christians earn the right to be heard, which opens the door to leading unsaved kids to Christ. Scott began to invest in a friendship with Steve, but Steve kept his eyes open, watching for hypocrisy or a hidden motive for Scott's friendship. He just couldn't fathom the thought that Scott would spend so much time with kids without having some other plan up his sleeve. Yet as he spent more and more time with Scott, he began to see the sacrifices that Scott was willing to make to invest in his life—and the lives of the other students—he slowly began to trust this new friend.

A Young Life to Remember

When the school year ended, Scott arranged a week at Saranac Village in upstate New York, for the kids who had been involved in Young Life that year. He invited Steve to join them on the trip. Steve, like any red-blooded high school boy, asked the most important question first, "What girls are going?" When he found out that one of the girls he was closest to planned on going to camp, he decided the trip might be worthwhile after all. All he needed to do was find the money to go. Fortunately, his Aunt Pauline and Uncle Russell came to the rescue and provided him with a gift that covered all the expenses.

Young Life promises that a camp week will be the best week of your life and the week that Steve attended was no exception. After the long bus ride to New York, he enjoyed a week of water skiing, parasailing, canoeing, volleyball, square dancing, mountain climbing, and more. Besides the activities during the day, woven throughout a Young Life camp week is the presentation of the gospel of Christ. Each night of the camp week, a different aspect of the gospel of Christ is presented to the kids. From who God is, to what Christ did for them on the cross, it is almost impossible for a student to walk away from a Young Life camp week without a clear understanding of the sacrifice made by Christ. One of the neatest parts of the camp week is a twenty-minute time of silence that the campers spend after hearing about the resurrection of Christ. Time alone with no distractions is such an oddity for many of these kids. For some, this was the time in which they began a relationship with Christ. After the twenty minutes, the camp had what they called a "Say So"—a moving experience in which those who had received Christ as their Savior would publicly stand up and proclaim their new relationship. Steve watched as many of the kids he had come to camp with had their "Say So."

While Steve was not one of the students to stand up that night, he was completely engaged with what the camp speaker had told him about Christ. The problem was he still felt very cynical inside. While others received Christ as their Savior, he prayed this prayer instead: "God, if You are real here at camp, You'll be just as real at home. Show me that You're real, and I'll trust You." It wasn't an arrogant prayer, but instead, the heart cry of a young man who had been let down and disappointed by the men in his life. Now, he was being asked to place his trust in a God that he wasn't sure was trustworthy.

Aren't you thankful that those are the types of prayers that God is eager to answer? Steve left camp that week unsaved, but open to seeing what God would show him. Well, God didn't wait long …

A New Beginning to Embrace

The bus ride back to Pennsylvania was long and hot, and the temperature in Chadds-Ford was hovering around 100 degrees. Steve arrived home early in the morning, but not early enough to catch his mom before she left for work. He would have to let himself into the condominium. Strangely, as Steve searched his pockets and then luggage, he couldn't find his house key, but he remembered that one window didn't latch tightly, so he prepared to break into his home. Steve's hand slipped as he was jiggling the window and his arm broke through the pane. As the glass shattered, a long shard pierced Steve's forearm and blood began to pulse in steady spurts from a major artery. As a neighbor heard the shattering glass and rushed to take him to the emergency room, Steve caught himself thinking this thought, "Is that you, God?"

Later that night, after being bandaged up and sent home, Steve would have his second encounter with the reality of God. For a couple of years, he had been in an on-and-off relationship with a female student. When he left for camp the week before, the relationship was in the "on" mode. Now, on his first night back from camp, he picked up his girlfriend and took her to the movies. They didn't talk much but he didn't really think that was so strange. In particular, they didn't utter a word about Saranac or any of the things he had learned there. When he drove her home that night, she turned to him and bluntly stated, "You've become a religious fanatic, and I never want to see you again!" With that, she got out of the car and walked out of Steve's life forever. (That's really okay by me!) Although he was stunned, again Steve's first thought was, "Is that you, God?"

On his first day home from camp, after praying that God would show Himself real, Steve was forced to look at what was most important in his life and the fact that he could lose those "most important" things at any time. First, he faced his own mortality, a theme that God has used repeatedly in Steve's life, as he watched the blood spurt from his arm and felt his knees go weak. Second, his most prized possession, his girlfriend, was gone … just like that. God was getting his attention.

Steve spent the next couple of weeks watching for "God-sightings," and on August 13, 1978, he was finally ready to surrender his life to the Lord. In the driveway of a friend's house, he prayed with Scott Hamilton to receive Jesus Christ as his personal Savior. Once done, Steve had no doubt about his salvation, but that was in August and in September, he headed off to college. A new believer, but with no firm foundation to build upon, the next couple of years would test his commitment and force him to take a stand, once and for all, for Christ.

Chapter 3

A Line in the Sand

College was another one of those "You Can't" episodes for Steve. His mother had no expectations, or even ambitions, for her only son to attend college. She had done her best to instill a diligent work ethic in Steve, and her fondest hope was that he would someday have a "steady" job, much like her duties at the railroad. Steve, however, had discovered that he actually liked learning, and he wanted to go further than high school.

Although Marion didn't stop Steve from going to college, she certainly didn't encourage him. At one point, when Steve had worked all day to fill out a long and laborious college application, he went out for a date and came home to find that same application in the trash. His mother hadn't bothered to look at the paperwork and just threw it away. Despite this type of discouragement, Steve persevered and was accepted to Earlham College in Richmond, Indiana.

Because of his late birthday, a still just seventeen-year old Steve loaded up his car and took off for Indiana. There he was, a brand-new believer who was about to attend a Quaker college. Although he assumed that this type of experience would encourage his newfound faith, Steve's short time at Earlham turned out to be a real eye-opener. Not only was he *not* challenged to grow in his Christian walk, he found himself pressured to participate in activities that he knew just weren't acceptable. So after one semester, Steve packed his car again and headed back to Pennsylvania.

He moved back in with his mom and spent the next semester taking classes at the University of Delaware. As well, he reconnected with Scott Hamilton and became involved in Young Life once more, this time as a leader and guitar player. Very quickly, Scott began to encourage Steve to put together Bible teaching to present at the Young Life Club. Being forced to accurately teach the Scripture to others forced Steve to grow very quickly himself.

One of the best things that the Young Life ministry did, for both Steve and me, was to instill in us a recognition of our obligation to serve the Lord. As soon as we came to know the Lord, we were encouraged to become leaders in a Young Life club and then, to begin to disciple believers that were even newer in their faith than we were. I remember, as a young Christian, meeting with my Young Life area director to study the Bible on Mondays, then meeting with a high school student on Tuesdays to teach her what I had just learned the day before. Week after week, I stayed one step ahead of the girl that I was mentoring. The responsibility and accountability I felt to present the bible accurately forced me to take my own walk with the Lord very seriously. As well, this commitment to ministry caused Steve and me to grow and realize that service for the Lord was a privilege; not a "favor" that we did for the Lord, but an opportunity to show Him how thankful we were for what He had done for us. That commitment to serve has never left us and we have always looked for ways to get involved and minister to others.

From Sinking-Sand to Solid Ground

After a semester at home, a now spiritually well-grounded Steve was more prepared to head off to school with a firm foundation in the Lord. This time, he enrolled in Clarion State College in Clarion, Pennsylvania. Although Clarion is a small school, Steve loved it there and made many close friends. While at Clarion, he and some other Christians spent time traveling to and ministering in local churches. They would lead music, sing specials, and preach the Word of God. God was beginning to prepare Steve for public ministry.

During his time at Clarion, Steve also learned how to lead others to the Lord. One of Steve's closest friends at Clarion was a young lady named Lisa. Lisa didn't know the Lord as her personal Savior, but because of their close friendship, one week she agreed to accompany Steve to church. During the service, Steve noticed that Lisa seemed stunned. As he questioned her about what she was thinking, Lisa shared with Steve what a shock it had been for her to see men actually singing and participating in the worship service. Her limited exposure to church had convinced her that church was something for women and children. The testimony of those faithful men was what began to draw Lisa's heart to the Lord and Steve was then able to share the gospel with Lisa. Shortly thereafter, she committed her life to Christ and she still serves Him faithfully, in full-time ministry, today.

Steve's involvement with other Christians and the time he was spending in the Word of God was building a deeper hunger for spiritual things. God was beginning the process of filling Steve's lamp with oil as He taught him to lead Bible studies and to facilitate worship services. Steve didn't know then where the Lord would eventually lead him, but he did know that his relationship with the Lord was the number one priority in his life. No longer was Steve content to have the Lord simply be a part of his life, instead, he was learning to focus everything around the Lord. Just as importantly, he was learning how to allow the Lord to guide and direct him.

The Economics of Happiness

Although he loved his time at Clarion, finances forced Steve to move home to Chadds-Ford, once again. This time he enrolled at West Chester University, the local college, and pressed on to receive his degree.

Today, Steve is an airline pilot, conference speaker, pastor, Navy Commander, and writer. You might be surprised to learn that his Bachelor's degree is in Economics. When he started college, he wasn't sure what he wanted to major in so he just took basic freshman level classes. Early in that first semester, he took his first Economics 101 exam. When the professor handed back the exam papers, Steve never received his test. Instead, the professor announced that he would be using Steve's test as the answer key because he had received a 100 percent. An economics major was born! Sadly, the rest of Steve's economic classes were a lot more challenging, but he persevered and earned his degree.

I could have warned him about economics. I have a degree in Communications. One semester, my Communications advisor convinced me to take an economics class … pass/fail. That is the only class I ever failed in my life! Actually, I was already dating Steve when I took the class but by the time I came to him, desperate for help, it was too late! He tried his best to teach me what the smiley faces and frowny faces on the economics graph meant, but to no avail. I still glaze over when he tries to explain the underlying details of our economic woes.

Back in Pennsylvania and enrolled at West Chester, Steve once again became involved in the local high school Young Life ministry. His life was fairly routine and calm, but little did he know what was coming. In the spring of 1982, I walked into his life and things began to change.

In March of 1982, I was a sophomore at West Chester University. I had come to college from York, Pennsylvania, hoping to play tennis and get an English degree. Although I had broken my ankle my senior year of high school, I felt confident that once I got to college I would be busy competing in tennis and studying hard. Unfortunately, that ankle kept breaking, over and over, and suddenly the athletics that had kept me in line all through high school were no longer there to keep me out of trouble. Forgetting that whole, "studying hard" part, I wholeheartedly embraced the college partier experience. For about a year and a half my tagline was "It's happy hour somewhere."

Back in York, when I was still in high school, I had attended Young Life and heard the gospel. One night, the speaker had made the point that if you didn't say "yes" to accepting Christ as your Savior, you were actually saying "no." I knew I didn't want to say that, so I raised my hand and made a verbal commitment to Christ. I say a verbal commitment, because nothing had changed in my heart; I was still just as lost, as ever. Nevertheless, because I had said the words, I thought I was a Christian.

Taming a Restless Heart

Now, here I was in college and living the party life. Too often, I found myself sitting on a barstool, telling someone that they should become a Christian because then they could be "just like me." *OUCH!* Thankfully, God sent a Christian friend my way. She was disgusted by my antics and told me so, right to my face! She told me that she never wanted to hear me tell another soul that I was a Christian because my life was an embarrassment to her Lord. Talk about a wake up call! In addition, she gave me this annoying little tract that just wouldn't go away. Every time I tossed that tract, entitled *This Is Your Life,* another one would appear.

Finally, in March, I picked up the tract and read it. I felt as though someone had written that tract about me. It laid out the life of a hypocrite; someone who looked one way, but actually lived another. I was crushed. That night, I prayed to God and asked Him to forgive me for the way I was living and the choices I had been making. I asked Him to take control of my life. That night I truly understood what it meant to be a child of God.

Two weeks later, I was at my first Young Life leader's meeting. Remember, I told you they got us involved in ministering quickly! Steve's memory of that night is of a blonde, wearing a yellow buttoned down shirt and docksides walking through the door. His first thought, "I wonder if that's who I'm going to marry?" (Of course, that was his first thought about every new girl.) My memory of that night is walking through the door and realizing that there was a dark haired young man, (Steve) sitting next to a really cute blond boy. My first thought, *I wonder if the blond has a girlfriend?* Hey, I was a brand new Christian and he was the first cute Christian boy I'd seen!

In a nutshell, that was the extent of our first meeting. The semester ended and Steve headed back to Saranac Village. Instead of being a camper, this time he spent the summer working as an assistant cook. It was there that Steve began to learn the important lesson of: You don't have to like it; you just have to do it. He also learned to cook camp-style. What's that? Camp-style cooking is *big* cooking. Nothing is made in small batches; more is better, and lots of food is the goal. A few years later, when Steve and I were first married, my job as a daycare teacher meant that I would arrive home after Steve. Of course, Steve wanted to be a good husband, so he offered to take over some of the evening cooking. Steve was and is a great cook, but remember, he learned camp cooking. Whenever he made dinner, we ate the leftovers for days! Yummy food, but lots of it!

While Steve was off serving the Lord and teenagers at the Young Life camp, I was having an adventure of my own. Much like Steve's semester at Earlham College, I was finding how hard it was to live the Christian life in an environment where I was the only Christian. After the semester ended, I had moved to Rehoboth Beach, Delaware, to spend my summer working at a pizza joint. In the beginning, I had great intentions to live faithfully for the Lord, but that didn't last long. Jeremiah 17:9 reminds us that our hearts are desperately wicked and can deceive even us. My summer became one heart deception after another.

I began the summer with great intentions of having a daily time with the Lord. After work each day, I would jump on my bike and ride out to the tip of the beach to spend time reading my bible. The second week of the summer, my bike pack, with my Bible in it, was stolen from my bicycle. Here came rationalization number one. I convinced myself that God knew how hard it was for me spend that time with Him after working all day, so He orchestrated the theft to let me know that I could take the summer off from Bible reading. Rationalization number two was even more bogus. I noticed that when I didn't go along and do the things that my summer roommates were involved in, they would get annoyed or frustrated with me. I rationalized that by causing them frustration, I was actually losing my ability to witness to them. Therefore, I decided to just go along with the crowd so that I could share Christ with my friends. Since I never said a word about the Lord, I'm not exactly sure how I thought that was going to happen.

By the end of the summer, I was totally disgusted with myself. I felt like a failure as a Christian, and I wasn't even sure how to get back on track. God had the answer to that dilemma and His answer was named Steve Scheibner. *Yikes!*

Remember, in the spring I had seen Steve, without really noticing him, at a Young Life leadership meeting. Steve, however, had remembered who I was. I returned to West Chester in August to begin my job as a resident assistant in the dorms. One evening, as I was showering, another RA came in the bathroom to tell me that someone named Steve was waiting in the lobby to talk to me. *Steve who? My on-again, off-again high school boyfriend was also named Steve?* I wondered if he had shown up at West Chester to surprise me. I quickly finished my shower, threw on my clothes, and hurried out to the lobby, only to find the dark-haired young man from the previous spring.

I was excited to meet Steve and even more excited that he had sought me out. Steve, on the other hand, was now looking at a girl who had spent a rough summer of late night partying at the beach. In the spring, I had been a pretty normal looking fair-haired, blue-eyed Irish girl. Over the summer, I had butchered my hair and spiked it up to look like Pat Benatar and now I wore all black. Steve could hardly believe that I was the same girl. Really, I was, but I had taken on the hard exterior that went with the life I had been living.

Steve was a gentleman, so instead of running away, he asked me to join a group of Young Life leaders at a local hangout, that night. After spending several hours talking to each other, I walked away from the evening smitten and began to tell my friends that I had met the man I was going to marry. Steve, however, walked away from our evening announcing to all his friends that he would "never date Megan Pierce"—one of many lines that Steve had drawn in the sand, another recurrent theme in his life.

Those first couple of months after I returned to school, I really struggled to be faithful in my Christian life. My old lifestyle at the beach was a constant temptation. One day, I cut all my classes and headed back to the beach to spend twenty-four hours with my old friends. What a mistake! I returned to college, the next day, looking horrible and feeling terribly guilty. West Chester was a good-sized university, but as I headed across campus that afternoon there was no one in sight except, you guessed it, Steve Scheibner. Worse yet, he was headed straight toward me with a big smile and his Bible under his arm. I couldn't keep it in and spilled my guts about the previous 24 hours. Steve didn't scold me (much), but he did encourage me to decide who I was going to be. Would I be a follower or Christ, or a follower of the world? I took his challenge to heart.

For whatever reason—I like to think it was the intervention of God—Steve continued to get to know me, and we soon became best friends. Once I was away from my beach friends, the old softer, sweeter Megan reemerged and Steve and I quickly realized that we saw life through the same, somewhat warped lens. Much like the Shaners, I was someone who loved words and language. Steve and I soon found ourselves engaged in vicious pun wars and battles of wit. The same things made us laugh and we were united in our commitment to let others see who we really were, on the inside. It bothered both of us to watch our Christian friends live one life at Young Life leadership and another life on campus.

Although none of our friends would believe it, Steve and I were not dating. We had just found a kindred spirit in one another and we loved spending time as friends. More importantly, for me, Steve was beginning to use some of that oil that God had put in his lamp. Early in our friendship, Steve asked me to do a Bible study with him at 5:00 a.m. I thought he was crazy! But, he knew that I needed to learn to sacrifice my comfort if I was ever going to get serious about my walk with the Lord.

Steve encouraged me to memorize my first memory verses and then helped me to get them done. Steve taught me to keep a prayer journal and challenged me to build a consistent prayer life. Steve took me to scripture and showed me that my first 10 percent belonged to God. He was my friend but even more, he was becoming my teacher.

Now, to be totally honest, I hadn't given up on my dream of being Mrs. Stephen Scheibner. More than once, I had scrawled that title in my notebook. Once, to my horror, Steve saw what I had written. But fortunately for me, he didn't mention it. I knew that Steve didn't think of me as a girlfriend, and I didn't want to jeopardize our friendship, so I put those hopeful thoughts on hold. After six months of friendship though, something happened to change our status quo.

All or Nothing

The second semester of my junior year, I had given up my RA job and moved into an apartment with the Young Life staff woman. Now, she was getting married and all of the Young Life leadership was invited. I just assumed that my best friend, Steve Scheibner, and I would be attending together, but about ten days before the wedding, he informed me that he had invited someone else. Remember Lisa from his Clarion University days? It seemed they had dated back then and she was going to be in town for the wedding.

I'd been fine with my friendship with Steve for many months, but there hadn't been any other girls, then. This felt like a new and unpleasant development. Acting quickly, I invited an old boyfriend to escort me to the wedding. I'd dated this young man my sophomore year and although he was very good looking, there just wasn't any spark between us.

The wedding day arrived and both Steve and I showed up with our respective dates. Lisa was a sweet girl, but I could see that she and Steve would drive each other crazy-I wasn't worried. Steve, on the other hand, took one look at Dave and began to stew. It got even worse when Dave and I left the wedding early. The next morning I received a call from Steve telling me that it was time for us to have a serious talk.

The gist of the serious talk was that Steve thought we should start dating and that if we were going to date; he thought it would be best if we didn't see other people. Now, that was exactly what I wanted to hear, but there was one small problem. Since up to that point, Steve and I were just friends, not dating, I had agreed to go on a date with my old boyfriend, Steve, from high school. I told Steve Scheibner about this little hiccup and he assured me that "It was no big deal". I think the easygoing way he received the news should have been my first hint of trouble.

At seven o'clock that evening, I opened my apartment door to greet my high school sweetheart, Steve. Instead, I found myself face to face with Steve Scheibner. As I stammered out, "What are you doing here?" he smiled a wicked grin and announced, "I'm coming along!" Which he did … for the entire date. *Awkward!* My poor high school boyfriend never knew what hit him. His well-thought-out plans for a sweet reunion were thwarted by a very determined Steve Scheibner.

Steve and I were so excited about our new dating relationship. Of course, we wanted to tell all of our friends. They, however, disappointed us by insisting that we had been dating all along. We knew they were wrong, but no one would believe us. After awhile, we just stopped protesting.

Steve and I started dating in March of 1983. He had graduated from West Chester in December of 1982. That year had been another rough time in the American economy. Steve worked some part-time jobs, but full-time employment was elusive. The only person hiring was Ronald Reagan and he was busy building up the Armed Forces. In March, the week after our big "announcement," Steve joined the United States Navy. In fact, our first official date was a visit to Philadelphia, where I witnessed him taking his initial Oath of Office. We finished off our date that evening by seeing the popular movie "Gandhi." Neither of us knew how Gandhi died and it only further cemented our relationship when we realized that we were both rooting for him to die so that the movie could end. You see, we'd begun holding hands in the first five minutes of the world's LONGEST movie and it seemed a bit awkward to let go. Thus, his death was necessary for us to gain our freedom from extremely sweaty palms. No disrespect to Gandhi intended but we were both anxious for the end of the movie!

Four months later, Steve and I were engaged and he was preparing to leave for Aviation Officer Candidate School. He'd spent the summer bulking up physically and memorizing scripture to prepare spiritually for whatever was to come. I still had a year of college to finish so our wedding was put on hold until the next July.

Our engagement was really true to our quirky personalities. Steve and I were working together at a Young Life camp and the night before Steve planned to propose, I tried to break up with him. I knew that he was leaving for the Navy in a short while and I figured it would be easier if I ended the relationship, before he did. Of course, Steve wasn't thinking about breaking up, he already had an engagement ring waiting back at home. He asked me to hold that whole breaking-up thought for a bit, and we would talk more the next day.

We left camp with a busload of teenagers and drove fourteen hours to get home. Steve's sister, Linda, was in town and he asked me to come over that evening to meet her. When I arrived, he pointed to Linda, said, "That's my sister," then rushed me out of the house. We went to a favorite spot of his, Longwood Gardens. Longwood Gardens is a lush botanical park, and in the summer, they have water shows. On this particular evening, they planned to shoot off fireworks, as well. We pulled up to the giant metal gate and were told that the garden was sold out; we couldn't enter. Not to be deterred, Steve drove to the back of the gardens, where he and his buddies used to climb the fence. Someone must have told on all those fence-climbers, because there was a guard in place to block our way. Disappointed, we sat along the highway and watched the fireworks.

We drove back to Steve's mother's condominium and I told Steve goodnight. I was exhausted from the camp trip and just wanted to go to bed. He begged me to take a walk and finally, I agreed. We walked down to the nearby pond and I sat down on a large rock. Steve told me that he had something to say. He dropped to one knee and told me that he loved me. *Uh-oh,* I knew what was coming next. Month's earlier Steve had told me that he would never tell another girl that he loved her, unless he was ready to follow up those words with a proposal. Sure enough, with his next words, he asked me to marry him. Remember, I had just tried to break up with him the night before! He told me that he understood if I needed to pray about the decision.

I don't know what came over me, but I asked if I could keep the ring while I prayed. Believe me, I've heard about that one for years! When Steve finished laughing, I said yes, and he slid a ring on my finger.

Steve designed my engagement ring. It is a single diamond in the middle, which represents God and His purity, surrounded by two rubies, one on each side, representing us, covered in Christ's blood. How could I say no to a story like that? When, years later, we began having children, Steve had a diamond placed in my wedding band for each birth. When our children became Christians, we had a ruby placed in his wedding band. The rings have been a great way to record our family history, and when our son, Peter, designed his wife's ring, he borrowed parts of our story.

So, now we were engaged, but Steve still had to leave for the Navy. Once again, he packed his faithful car and off he drove. This time he was headed to Pensacola, Florida, and a Marine drill instructor. He never could have imagined the lessons that God would teach him during that time, but as always, God was faithfully preparing Steve for what would come later in his life. The oils of patience, perseverance, honor, courage, and commitment, were steadily increasing the fuel level in Steve's lamp. Lessons that seemed like "just part of the job," would later build the spiritual muscle that Steve would need to persevere in ministry. The process was speeding up.

Chapter 4

Borrowed-Time Believers

Although Steve's mom loved him dearly, she was never a very involved mother. Her busy work and social schedule meant that she and Steve spent limited time together and from a very young age he had become used to making his own decisions. The moment he entered NAS Pensacola on October 28, 1983, that free and easy way of life would be a fond memory from his past.

Aviation Officer Candidate School took Steve's breath away. From the wake-up call of a metal trash can being thrown down the hall at 5:00 a.m. each day, to the constant yelling and name-calling, nothing could have prepared him for this period in his life. His time was not his own, his activities were not his own, even his thoughts were not his own. He was forced to learn a new language, (Navy Lingo) and to submit completely to the chiseled Marine barking orders in his face. Everyday he wanted to quit, but he would tell himself, "Just one more day;" he, "Just-One-More-Day'd," himself the whole way through that program.

Our engagement pictures show Steve with a full thick head of dark hair. That was about to be the first major change in his life. AOCS began quickly with haircuts for the new Officer Candidates. Steve watched as the line in front of him rapidly diminished with one new Candidate after another buzzed to the scalp. To add to the stress, each one was turned to face the other men for his haircut; building the anticipation and dread of what was coming for them. Just how many men dropped out after having their heads shaved shocked Steve. This was 1983 and no one had a shaved head back then. Just the thought of having to come home bald helped Steve to stick it out those first few days.

Early in AOCS, the men were given a talk by one of the marine drill instructors. This man told them to look to their left and then to their right. He then told them that at least one of the men next to them would not make it through AOCS. There it was, another "can't" statement. Steve determined he would stay the course and complete his training. His class started with seventy-two men and ended with twenty-eight. Steve would be one of the remaining.

The whole point of AOCS was to push the Candidates to the breaking point; to make them feel as though they couldn't take it for one more moment. Steve was pushed harder than he'd ever been pushed in his life. Little privileges became very important to him. I remember when he was finally able to call me for the first time and he was bubbling over with excitement because his Class had earned the privilege of chocolate milk for lunch!

A Lesson in Humility

The drill instructors made it their goal to teach these young men discipline, because discipline would be what was needed to become competent Naval Aviators. For Steve, his social personality would often get him into trouble. One day, he was marching into the chow hall with his class when he made the unfortunate mistake of catching eyes with a drill instructor. He knew that his eyes were supposed to be glued to the head of the Candidate in front of him but it was just too tempting to look around and see what else was going on in the chow hall. He learned an important lesson that day, but I'm afraid the drill instructor learned a lesson too, a lesson about putting Steve in the limelight.

Steve was instructed to stand on a chair, point to himself, and yell out loudly, "Hey, look at me! I'm undisciplined!" Obediently, Steve stepped up on the chair and began to do as instructed. Remember though, Steve loves acting and drama. Soon, he was throwing his arms up dramatically and turning like a lighthouse as he pointed to himself and chanted, "Hey … Look At Me … I'm Undisciplined!! Hey … Look At Me … I'm Undisciplined!!" The drill instructor quickly realized that Steve was enjoying the attention just a little too much and yanked him down off the chair.

Steve's physical and spiritual preparations served him well as he progressed through AOCS, and the training he received there helped him to be mentally prepared to competently deal with the daily challenges he would face as a Naval Aviator. After four long months, Steve was ready to graduate from AOCS and receive his commission as an Ensign in the United States Navy.

The Stuff Heroes Are Made Of

The day before he received his commission, one of his most respected drill instructors shared a challenge that would stick with Steve for the rest of his life. This man had spent time in Vietnam. While there, he led a squad of very young marines—guys who had only one job: Go behind enemy lines and retrieve pilots who had been shot down. When they set off on their missions, they had no idea whether or not the pilot was still alive—or even whether the pilot had been captured. Regardless, these young men felt as if they had the most important job in the world, and they performed their duties wholeheartedly. The drill instructor went on to share this sobering truth with the Candidates. He said, "I know that for every pilot that we go in to save, I will lose two Marines." Whether the pilot was dead or alive, two young Marines would sacrifice their lives and these Marines considered it an honor to do so. The drill instructor continued, "We will always make the trip to come and save you. The question you have to answer is this: Are you worth the trip?" For Steve, that question immediately became a defining goal in his life. He determined that regardless of the circumstances in his life, he would be worth the trip.

All that day, the drill instructor's admonition kept running through his mind. He thought of all those young Marines who were willing to sacrifice their lives for unknown, perhaps undeserving, pilots. What did it mean to be worth the trip? As he pondered that question, God brought a clear realization to his mind. On the cross, Jesus Christ had made the trip for him, Steve Scheibner, when He already knew that Steve was totally undeserving of the trip. Steve wasn't unknown to Christ. The Lord already knew the sinful state of Steve's heart and still He gladly made the trip to the cross out of faithful obedience to His Father. It was then that Steve began to truly understand what it meant to have someone die in his place. For him, it was the initial step in becoming a "Borrowed-Time Believer." Steve caught a glimpse of the urgency of living life on purpose and of focusing only on bringing glory to God. Seventeen years later, God would take the events of September 11, 2001, and use them to firmly plant Steve's feet on the road of the Borrowed-Time Believer. It was then, that the initial flame of urgency that had been ignited in AOCS would become a blazing fire consuming Steve's life.

The following day, Steve received his commission as an Ensign in the United States Navy. Steve's mom and I traveled to Pensacola, together, to attend his commissioning service. I don't think Marion was ever more proud of her son and she delighted to tell all of her friends about her boy, the Ensign. For me, it was my first introduction to the military world, a way of life that would become the centerpiece for our family for the next twenty-eight years.

Finding His Fit

The next step for Steve would be flight school, where he thought that he would be training to be a Navigator. Steve had entered AOCS as a candidate in the Navigator program, but all through his training he had toyed with the idea of transitioning to the pilot program. He had the prerequisite 20/20 vision and had only agreed to be a navigator because that was what the recruiter talked him into doing. He prayerfully began the process to transition to the pilot program.

Transitioning wasn't impossible but it wasn't a guarantee, either. We didn't know then how God would use Steve's job as a pilot to further His Kingdom and His plans for Steve. To us, being a pilot just seemed more in line with Steve's personality. Pilots are idea guys; the kind of people who can't resist flipping switches and pushing buttons, even when they don't know the intent of the switches or buttons. Navigators, on the other hand, are much more stable. These are the people who always do their homework and keep their pencils sharpened. Steve had some definite pilot tendencies!

Steve made it all the way through the lengthy transition process and finally entered the last office to get the last signature. There he met LCDR

Lugg. In the spirit of Mrs. McWilliams, LCDR Lugg told Steve that he would *never* make it as a pilot. Although he finally signed the necessary paperwork, LCDR Lugg bet Steve his next paycheck that Steve would wash out of the pilot training program within a couple weeks. Another "can't" statement, but by now Steve was unfazed by that type of discouragement. He went on to earn his Wings of Gold and we have yet to see that paycheck that LCDR Lugg promised to Steve. Twenty-eight years, thousands of military sorties, qualifications on countless aircrafts, twelve-thousand-plus hours, and FAA check rides galore, again, like Mrs. McWilliams, LCDR Lugg was wrong!

Golden Wings or a Wedding Ring?

The lessons of patience and perseverance that Steve was learning in AOCS would serve him well in our relationship. As Steve was progressing and succeeding in the Navy, our engagement was hitting some major rough spots. Areas that needed to be discussed and dealt with were continually being swept under the rug, by both of us, with the understanding that we would take care of them after the wedding. As more and more of these problematic areas surfaced, I became more and more unsettled. I knew that Steve was being stretched to the breaking point, but I couldn't proceed with wedding plans while I had so many unanswered concerns.

In November of that year, I broke off our engagement. I flew to Florida to see Steve in person and to return the ring. We both knew that we loved each other, but we also both knew that our relationship needed some work before we could go forward with a wedding. What's more, we were both serious about our walks with the Lord and we were determined to make sure that our decisions for the future were in alignment with the Word of God and that they would bring God glory. Even though we were young believers, we realized that the wedding was just a day, while the marriage needed to last forever. As soon as I broke off the engagement, my parents, who were not Christians, removed their blessing from our relationship and encouraged me to move on with my life.

After three months of deep talks and steadfast prayer, Steve and I felt ready to move forward with our wedding and life together. However, now we had a problem. We were committed to honoring my parents, even though they weren't Christians, and they no longer supported our marriage. At one point, they told us they would know we truly loved each other if we went against their wishes. Tempting, but we knew that in order to honor God and my parents, we just couldn't do that. We waited patiently, and six weeks later they called to say that they had changed their minds. The wedding was back on the calendar.

Sometimes, the process of God pointing oil in the lamp isn't pleasant. In fact, sometimes it just plain hurts. Hebrews 12:11 reminds us that no discipline seems pleasant at the moment and having to end our engagement certainly felt like unpleasant discipline. At the time, I just couldn't see how something so hurtful could bring about any good fruit. Breaking off the engagement was one of the hardest things that I had ever had to do. There were times I wondered why God didn't just let us have a smooth engagement and excited backing by my parents. However, as our lives have taken us down the path of counseling many young couples, our experience has proven invaluable. More than once, we have had to tell a couple that we didn't believe that they were ready to be married, or even that they should get married. Knowing that we went through a broken engagement in order to be spiritually prepared for marriage has only served to strengthen our testimony and counsel to these young couples. Additionally, we can strongly encourage couples to seek and wait for their parents' approval; they know that we practiced what we preach.

Time to Go in Tandem

Steve and I planned a simple wedding for July 7, 1984. In the meantime, he began flight training in Milton, Florida, and I finished my degree in Communications at West Chester University.

The day before Steve was to come home for our wedding was the first time he soloed in an airplane. Talk about pressure! Failing the flight meant he wouldn't be able to come home and the wedding would have been postponed, again. Thankfully, Steve has always been an excellent pilot, (*Good Stick* is the Navy term,) since the first moment he got into the cockpit, he aced the flight, and came rushing home for the wedding.

One little God moment happened on his way home. Steve flew home on American Airlines. When the crew found out that he was coming home for our wedding, they presented him with a bottle of champagne. Even though we don't drink, it was a sweet gesture. Years later, when Steve interviewed with American for a pilot job, they asked him what he liked about their company. With no hesitation, Steve was able to share how impressed he had been by the kindness of their employees. Even then, God was working behind the scenes to prepare Steve for his time at American.

We had a simple wedding in West Chester, loaded our gifts in my car, and started the drive back to Milton, Florida. Probably my favorite part of the whole wedding was the receiving line. Person after person went through the line, shook Steve's hand, and said something like this: "I thought you were never going to date Megan Pierce. She won!" That was one line in the sand drawn by Steve, but thoroughly erased by God! Because we had been trained by Young Life to minister and instructed by my Aunt Peg, a military wife, to always practice hospitality, within minutes of arriving in Milton, we began our married life by inviting all of our new neighbors into our apartment to share the top tier of our wedding cake. That early discipline of practicing hospitality has stayed with us to this day.

Flight training was a stressful time for Steve, with one check ride after another, but regardless, we really enjoyed our time in Milton. We quickly became involved in a good church and began leading the junior high youth group. After our Young Life training, not serving was never an option. Our time in Milton went quickly and within a few months, we were off to Corpus Christi, Texas, for Steve's final Flight School.

Once we arrived in Corpus, we sought out and met the Young Life Area director. Wayne and Debbie Smith became dear friends as we all served in Young Life together. As well, they became an example to us of what a Christian family looked like and how a Christian family functioned. Neither Steve nor I had grown up in homes that were centered on Christ and we loved to spend time at the Smith's, just watching how they treated one another and their children. Many of our early convictions about family life were initiated as we observed their family.

I had found work at a daycare center and being with other people's children all day was causing me to hate the idea of having children of our own. I grew up the youngest of three children and my sports schedule had meant that I didn't even baby-sit very often. Now, spending hours with unruly, undisciplined children was painting a terrible picture of parenthood for me. Being with Wayne and Debbie's kids showed me how different it could be when you were engaged in training your own children. Steve and I began to build convictions regarding how we would raise our children someday and we began to make plans for me to transition to a stay at home mom when our children finally did arrive.

The other life-changing thing that we were a part of in Corpus Christi was our first church plant. We attended a new church work that met in an elementary school. As we helped to set up chairs each week and as we met in member's homes for midweek activities, Steve and I had our first glimpse of the excitement of a new church. When it came time for Steve to become a church planter, we were thrilled and excited, not frightened and overwhelmed.

God was preparing us even then, but of course, we had no idea of His plans for the future. At that point, we thought that Steve would be a Navy pilot for twenty years, then retire and pursue whatever seemed interesting to him at that time. Obviously that was our plan, not God's.

I cried when it was time to leave Corpus Christi. We had made dear friends in our time there and we had felt useful in the Young Life ministry. It was hard to leave, but leaving was to become a normal part of our lives. For a girl who had lived in one house her whole life, the military lifestyle was a huge adjustment. However, in the same way that God was preparing Steve for his future ministry, He had been preparing me to be a suitable helper for Steve. Steve has always told people that he was proud of how adaptable I am. That adaptability is simply a gift from God. He is the one that has taught me not to hold onto people and places too tightly and for that, I am very thankful.

After Steve completed his flight training and received his coveted Wings of Gold, we received orders to our first duty station, Brunswick, ME. We had prayed that God would keep us on the East Coast and somewhat close to our families and that prayer was answered. Our first year and a half of marriage had been spent in flight training. Because we moved so often and because Steve was a full-time student, that first year or so felt somewhat like life was on hold. We felt more like students, or kids, than responsible adults. Yes, we were involved in church and made some really great friends, but in the back of our minds, there was always the realization that we would be leaving soon. Now it was time to move to Maine, buy our first house, settle into a church and a community, and finally, become adults. For God, Maine would become the place for us to develop clear convictions, strengthen our Bible understanding, and begin to use that oil that He had been pouring into our lives. We were about to learn what it meant to be responsible for someone other than ourselves.

Chapter 5

Life Objective: Glorify God

Sometimes, when Steve and I look back at the decisions we made as a young couple we often wonder, *What were we thinking?* We definitely had far more energy back then and that's a good thing, because some of our choices just made life way harder than it had to be. So it was with our first major decision in Maine.

Just about the time we received our verbal orders, telling us that we would be spending four-plus years in Maine, we found out about another unique opportunity. A church in Norway, Maine, was interested in doing a partnership with Young Life. They wanted to hire a part-time youth worker and pay them a full-time salary to do Young Life work, as well as leading the church youth program. It seemed like the perfect opportunity for me. We didn't have any children yet and Steve would be leaving a couple months after we arrived in Maine for his first deployment. I applied and interviewed for the job. A week after the interview, we received the call. I had been chosen from among several candidates to fill the position. Although Norway was an hour and a half from Brunswick, nothing seemed too hard if it meant an opportunity where we could serve the Lord.

Seeing Through the Lenses of Truth

That position in Norway began our training process in learning how to discern what is and isn't biblical. Up until that point, Steve and I had been fairly sheltered from doctrinal issues. We had always connected with the other Young Life leaders everywhere we lived and our mutual service and shared training had been the basis of our fellowship. The churches that we had attended all had adhered to basically the same Statements of Faith, and I think that, somewhat naively, we thought that when someone used the name *Christian,* they automatically believed the same things we believed.

Now, suddenly we were attending and I was on staff with a church that didn't hold to the same tenets of faith that we so strongly believed. The longer we were there, the more obvious the differences became. While we believed that "All must be saved," this church thought that making that type of commitment was optional and should definitely wait until adulthood. I was talking to high school kids about sin and the church was preaching, "Do your best, that's all God expects." I was encouraging kids to read their Bibles and to memorize Scripture; the church didn't even encourage the members to use the Bible for sermons. Steve left on deployment and our infrequent, but much anticipated phone calls became stressful times of trying to discern what to do.

Finally, our decision became clear. Even though the high school work was going very well and we had seen thirteen teens trust Christ as their Savior, it became obvious that I had to leave the job. The more we searched our Bibles, the more clear it became to us that doctrine was very important to God and therefore, it needed to be just as important to us. The teens and their parents couldn't believe that we would walk away from such a well-paid job, but our commitment to portraying Christ accurately made it clear that we must go. God was teaching us to dig a little deeper and to measure decisions against His Word, not against what seemed like a perfect opportunity.

God was using that time not only to build our commitment to His Word, but He was teaching us other important lessons, as well. We had never before faced judgment and anger because of our beliefs. When I handed in my resignation, we were faced with angry people, hate mail, and isolation. God was beginning to thicken our skin. That wasn't to be the last time that taking a stand for what we believed would earn us the dislike of folks who just didn't understand us. We left Norway, bought a new house, and found a church of like-minded believers.

Just about the same time, we found out that we were expecting our first child. From the beginning, we never had trouble recognizing that each child is a gift from God. When Steve had returned home from deployment, thirteen of the squadron wives had become pregnant at the same time. By the third month of our pregnancies, only four of us were still carrying babies. We learned quickly to be thankful for the child we were carrying.

Our new church provided us with many opportunities to grow. Fairly quickly, Steve and I were asked to take over the teen Sunday school and youth program. We loved those kids and loved opening our home to them. When Steve planted the church in Maine thirteen years later, several of those teens became faithful adult members.

Celebrating God's Gift of Life

April 3, 1987, brought massive flooding and the birth of our first baby girl, Kaitlyn Elizabeth Scheibner. Steve and I were both stunned by how beautiful she was. You see, we had spent months looking in the mirror and trying to envision my round face with his nose and my tiny ears and his narrow eyes … you get the picture. Instead, God had presented us with this lovely little girl. Our time with the Smith's in Texas and our study of the

Word of God had laid the foundation for our child-raising beliefs, now was the time to put that head knowledge into practice.

When we look back at some of the things that seemed so hard in our lives, it is easy to see God's hand at work. One month after Katie was born, Steve left on another six-month deployment. That seemed like such a hard thing at the time, but even then, God was beginning to prepare us, as a couple, for the lifestyle that His calling would hold for us. With Steve gone, I had to learn how to competently manage our home and make decisions not just for me now, but for our baby daughter, as well. It was important to me that Steve feel confident in my ability to cope while he was gone and those early lessons in taking my burdens to God, instead of saving them to hand to Steve during our bi-weekly phone calls, continues to bear great fruit, today.

As an added twist in the learning to cope process, God provided us with a surprise. Two months into Steve's deployment, we arranged for Katie and I to travel to Iceland for a two-week visit. Unfortunately, the week before our departure, the Commanding Officer of the squadron made a decree that no more children could visit the barracks. We were forced to make a decision. We had already committed to keeping our marriage as the primary relationship in our home, so we decided that I would still travel to Iceland while Katie stayed home with close friends. I knew that she would be well cared for, but it still meant leaving my baby and a sudden stop to nursing her.

One week into my visit to Iceland, I began to have some feelings that were strangely familiar. I told Steve, "I think we're having another baby!" He thought I was nuts, but to placate me, we bought a pregnancy test. When the negative sign appeared we thought I must have been imagining things. Three weeks later, I was home but still having those funny feelings. On my own now, I bought another pregnancy test, took it, and saw the negative sign once again. I headed off to church. Three hours later, when I returned from church, the negative sign was positive and I knew that baby number two was on the way! This baby was our son, Peter Warren. Peter has spent his life keeping us guessing, beginning with his one-month early birth during his father's first flight as a Mission Commander. Without a doubt, Peter was born bent on making his mark on the world! The film "In My Seat," is a part of that mark, but more about the film later.

Forming Our Life Objectives

By now, I was twenty-six years old and Steve was twenty-eight. We were still one of the youngest couples in the church, but God began to use us in ways that were unexpected. On a regular basis, Steve was beginning to be asked to speak to men's groups and to lead other men in Bible studies. At the same time, I was asked to teach the Ladies Sunday School, a class consisting mostly of women in their fifties, sixties, and seventies. What's more, I became the go-to person to share the devotional teaching at new mother's baby showers. I only had one baby when those requests began, so on paper, I sure didn't look like the obvious choice.

Although Steve and I were somewhat taken aback by those unexpected positions of responsibility, we had committed to saying, "Yes" when asked to serve, unless there was a clear and obvious reason that we needed to say, "No." Those opportunities provided us with the confidence and the foundation for the teaching that we still carry out, today.

That routine was to become the normalcy of our lives in the Navy. We attended church, taught Bible studies, opened our home to young people, and had babies. From Brunswick, Maine, we were transferred back to

Corpus Christi, Texas, and the life that had become so normal to us just continued, only this time in a new in a new location.

While we were in Corpus, we once again became part of a new church plant. Again, Steve was stockpiling ideas that he would use later when God called him to plant Cornerstone Baptist Church in Topsham, Maine. During that time, Steve went through an intensive discipleship program taught by our new pastor. It was during this training that Steve developed his life objective, a document that has served to guide him, and our family, in the decision making process for many years.

Steve's Life Objective goes like this: *To seek, trust, and glorify God, through humble service and continual prayer. To raise up qualified disciples as quickly as possible, so that some day I might hear God say, "Well-done my good and faithful servant."*

At the same time that he was developing his life objective, I was going through ladies discipleship and being encouraged to write my own. Mine goes like this: *To glorify God with my words, thoughts, and deeds, and to become a Godly older woman and wife of noble character, so I may be qualified to teach the younger women and therefore, not disgrace the name of God.*

Although our life objectives are vastly different, when you put them together, they form the cornerstone of our ministry through Characterhealth. We wrote those life objectives before we were thirty, but God was orchestrating, even then, how they would be fulfilled in our lives in 2011.

Along with the great training at our church, we were introduced to Precept Ministries. Steve and I were both trained to lead Precept Bible Studies and we have used that training everywhere we have gone. That Precept training, along with the Nouthetic counselor training that we received was essential in our teaching and counseling ministries within the church. Again, God was putting oil for future use in our lamps and we were soaking up every drop that we could get.

During our time in Corpus Christi, we were blessed with another daughter, Emily Marion, or Emma. Our home was always filled with college students and she spent her first year being held, tossed, and snuggled by young single men and women. Emma was our only child born in Texas and she still proudly proclaims herself a Texan. Also during that time, we opened our home to a troubled sixteen-year old student. She lived with us for several months while we spent time counseling with both her and her parents. It was a thrill for us when they reached the point that she could finally move back home with her parents. This was our first introduction to family ministry. Years later we relied on the lessons learned during that time as we began to minister to families through our church plant in Maine.

The end of our orders in Corpus signaled the end of Steve's obligation to the Navy, and it was decision time for our little family. Steve loved the Navy, but we had witnessed first-hand just how hard the deployments were on older children. After much prayer, he decided to end his time on Active Duty and to apply for a job with the airlines.

On a Wing and a Prayer

In 1990, all of the major airlines were hiring. We had been told by people in the know that Delta Airline was partial to hiring Christians. In fact, all of the Christians that we knew that applied to the airlines had been hired by Delta. Steve confidently sent his application off to Delta and waited for his interview call. We thought he was a shoe-in. He waited, and waited, and waited. Delta never did call us. Steve even applied a second time, but still

Delta showed no interest in interviewing him. We just couldn't understand what was going on, but God knew. If Steve had been hired by Delta, so many of the events that made up our next 21 years would have never happened. God knew then, how Steve's testimony from September 11th would be used to influence people, now.

While we waited to hear from the airlines, God gave us a great opportunity to learn more about trusting Him. Not only was Steve unemployed, but during that time of uncertainty, we found out that we were expecting baby number four. I'll never forget our phone call to my dad. When we shared our exciting news, he was certain that Steve had gotten an offer from the airlines. Instead, we told him that he was going to be a grandfather, again. I can only imagine what he was picturing in his mind, his unemployed son-in-law, pregnant daughter, and three young children, moving into his tiny split-level ranch. All he could do was stammer out numbers. "One, two, three ... four children, *oh my!*"

After what seemed like years, (it was really weeks,) Steve received a call from American Airlines. He interviewed and was hired to be a First Officer, based in New York City. The Navy was over, or so we thought, and we were ready to head off to the next chapter of our lives. Steve's new career was about to provide the paycheck that would allow God to continue to fill Steve's spiritual lamp with oil.

Chapter 6

Soaring to New Heights

Steve began his new job with American Airlines in December of 1991. We settled in the Lehigh Valley in Pennsylvania and began the adjustment to civilian life with no deployments and no more moves, or so we thought. Living in Pennsylvania meant that we were much closer to our parents and the children's grandparents. We were excited for them to really get to know their grandchildren.

In May of 1992, we welcomed our third daughter, Margaret Hannah, or Molly. Peter had been desperately hoping for a brother and he and Steve composed a birth announcement outlining his disappointment. A week after Molly's birth, our family and friends received an announcement stating: "Steve and Peter Scheibner regret to inform you ... it's another one of Them." Regardless of Peter's initial disappointment, the whole family adored little Molly with her crazy dark hair. Parenting Molly has been somewhat like parenting Lucille Ball or Carol Burnett. She is one of the most naturally comedic people I know, and her decision to declare a drama major in college came as no surprise to us.

A year and a half later, Nathaniel Pierce, (Nate) became Scheibner baby number five. By then, we'd stop announcing how many children we thought we would have and instead, we treated having children like any other decision we faced. We would spend time praying and trust that God would show us when it was time for another child. He'd shown Himself faithful in every other area, why not children? Nate was a total "go-with-the flow" baby, which was very helpful in our ever-growing household.

With a new home, came another new church. This time we settled our family at Heritage Baptist Church in nearby Schnecksville, PA. Filled with young home-schooling families, Heritage was a great fit for us. Although Heritage wasn't technically a church plant any more, it was still a fairly new work and it was an exciting time to be a part of the church. The pastor of Heritage had graduated from Calvary Baptist Seminary in Lansdale, Pennsylvania, and the church supported the seminary, as well. That seminary would soon become a very important part of our journey.

Fueling the Spark

One Sunday, shortly after arriving at Heritage, the church hosted a "Seminary Sunday." Several of the professors from the school came to Heritage that day to share their work. The Dean of the seminary presented the morning's sermon. Steve was very impressed with the institution's ministry and the obvious love for the Lord that was evidenced in the professor's lives. As we were leaving church that day, Steve off-handedly commented that he thought that he might like to take some seminary classes, maybe ... sort-of ... *someday.*

We headed to Chili's for lunch with the kids. "Coincidentally" (Really, God's timing,) the professors from the seminary had chosen the same restaurant for their lunch. Steve walked over to their table to thank them for their ministry at Heritage, that morning. He was gone for a loooong time! When he came back, he announced that he was going to begin seminary classes and that his first class was the next morning. Those professors didn't waste any time recruiting him! At first, Steve was just taking one or two classes a semester but soon he was hooked and couldn't get enough of the teaching.

Called and Committed

Steve was not your average seminary student. He was older than most of the students and found his peer friendships among the professors. His airline schedule meant that the seminary had to be very flexible in their dealings with him. Often, he would make a request that everyone was certain would be denied, only to receive a "yes" answer. I'm still not sure how he does it, but Steve just wins people over with his self-deprecating sense of humor.

About the same time, Steve rejoined the Navy as a Reserve Officer in Willow Grove, Pennsylvania. Steve had always stood out in his Active Duty squadrons for his exceptional flying skills and it was the same in Willow Grove. Soon, he was their Chief Instructor Pilot and the Check Pilot who was tasked with instructing the other instructors. Many days, he went straight from seminary to the Navy, or vice versa. The Navy was a great part-time job and Steve loved flying the P-3s. At the time, that's all we thought the Navy would ever be, just a great part-time job. Later, God would use Steve's Reserve job to become the foundation of the Characterhealth ministry, but all of that was still in the future. With American Airlines as his full-time job, seminary classes, and the Navy Reserves, Steve's life was busy, busy, and *busy!*

Our life at home was just as hectic. During Steve's five years in seminary, we added two more children to our family. Baleigh Grace was born in October of 1995 and Stephen Jr. followed on May 29, 1998. Their older siblings adored these two youngest children and they are still doted on to this day. Because we had made the decision to home school, it was possible for Steve to spend his off time investing in the children. From the beginning, Steve and I had worked hard to be very intentional in our child training. We wanted our children to love the Lord and our family and to be committed to embracing and living out excellent character. God really blessed our efforts and people began noticing and asking us what we were doing to produce such kind and obedient children. We began hosting parenting classes in our home. The basis of our parenting and home schooling was the Bible, so that was where we took the other parents, as well. Soon, it became necessary for us to begin organizing our thoughts and ideas into a workable format, and the first skeleton outline of Parenting Matters emerged.

Planting Ministry Seeds

The entire time that Steve was in seminary, people would ask him what he planned to do with his degree. Many years earlier, one of the lines that Steve had drawn in the sand was to announce that he would *never* become a pastor. With the end of seminary drawing near, God began to erase that line in the sand, as well. As Steve met with his professors, and especially with his close friend and the Dean of the seminary, Dave Burggraff, it became obvious that Steve's job as an airline pilot and the flexibility that it afforded him made for the perfect church planting situation. Because Steve could only work for a certain number of days at the airline each month, he would have plenty of time to establish a new work. What's more, with the airline paying his salary, the problem of raising money for a new pastor would be avoided and a new church could invest in ministry items instead of putting all of their money toward a pastor's salary. For our entire ten years at Cornerstone, Steve's salary at American Airlines paid our bills.

All of his years of training, both in the Navy and in seminary, as well as his faithfulness in his walk with the Lord had prepared Steve for this opportunity. He began to bubble over with ideas and we, as a family, began to pray that God would show us where the church plant should be.

The summer before Steve's seminary graduation, friends of ours from Maine contacted us. They had been in the same church for many years and felt that God was showing them that it was time for a change. We'd lived in that area of Maine and we knew that their choices were limited. The note they sent us went on to explain that they were praying that Steve would consider coming back to Maine to plant a church. God was answering our prayers.

The entire next year was one answered prayer after another. Our very old farmhouse sold before we ever put it on the market. The grange in Topsham, Maine, became available and we were able to rent it to begin having worship services. Dear friends from Pennsylvania decided to join us and moved their family to Maine to assist with the new work. Very importantly, Steve's job with American Airlines opened up a pilot spot in Boston, just the very month that we were moving. He had been willing to commute to New York, but Boston made life so much easier. As well, Steve was able to transfer his Navy Reserve job up to Brunswick, Maine. Now he was back flying P3s where he had started flying them in the first place. God was putting all of the pieces in place.

Expanding Our Borders

In that final year before we left Pennsylvania, God had one more, very important, lesson to imprint in our minds. In the summer of 1999, I had been spending some time in a home-school chat room. One day, a young mother posed a question, basically asking if we could do harm to our children by sheltering them from the real world. I answered her post, explaining my belief that we shelter our children while they are young, in order to prepare them to minister to the "real world" when they are spiritually mature and ready. To us, sheltering really meant preparing and strengthening.

The next day, I heard from the young mother again. But now, she revealed that although, yes, she was a young mother, she was also a reporter for the *New York Times Magazine*. The truth was that she was fishing for some quotes to use in an article that she was writing about Michael Farris, the then-President of Home School Legal Defense. (HSLDA) The writer's name was Margaret Talbot, and she asked if we would consider allowing her to visit us for a day to observe our family and to ask some questions about home schooling. Steve and I prayed about the decision and agreed to have her come to our house. She drove down from New York, with her husband and son, and spent a day watching our family and casually asking questions. When she left, we assumed that was the end of our involvement with the article. We couldn't have been more wrong.

Three months later, I received a phone call from a professional photographer. He told me that he wanted to come and spend an entire weekend with our family, taking posed and spontaneous photos. We were a bit confused; a whole weekend seemed like overkill for a few quotes in someone else's article. When we questioned the photographer, he told us that the article had changed direction and was now a 10,000-word piece that was completely focused on our family. We contacted Margaret who somewhat sheepishly told us that yes; the article was now about us.

In February of 2000, there we were, adorning the front cover of the *New York Times Magazine*. It is hard to describe the myriad emotions that we felt, looking at ourselves in full color and reading the title, *Inward Christian Soldiers*. Margaret had tried to make a point about our family, but she just couldn't make it stick. The whole time she was trying to paint a picture of isolation. However, the article talked about the people who spent time in our home, the ministries we were involved in, and the way that people were attracted to our children. By including a copy of a letter that Peter had written to Senator Rick Santorum, Margaret included the entire gospel message, which Peter had written out for the Senator. An inclusive God shone through the article and for that we were thankful.

Regardless, the *New York Times Magazine* circulates, in general, to a population that is not friendly to Christians or conservatives. That article generated the most response they had ever received from a cover story, both good and bad. While some people respected the intentional way that we were raising our family, others hated that we didn't just go along with the societal flow. One letter to the editor was particularly scathing.

While the photographer had been taking the pictures of our family one morning, the temperature had dropped dramatically. He was bundled in a heavy winter coat, but our family had to stand outside coatless for an hour, while he took photo after photo. Unbeknownst to us, our children had slipped their cold, little hands up inside their sleeves, to keep them warm. The picture on the front cover of the magazine shows six children with no hands. One reader of the magazine looked at that photo and made a swift and harsh judgment. He wrote to the editor stating that the children's hidden hands clearly portrayed the repression that they felt in our home. He went on to call the nation to pray that the Scheibner children would rebel and escape one day. Letters like that took some explaining to our children. It was a great opportunity to teach them about seeking to know the context of any given situation. Still, the harsh words were hurtful to their little hearts.

God was definitely preparing us for what was to come later in our lives. In the same way that some people responded so strongly and hatefully toward the New York Times article, we have seen people respond the same way toward the "In My Seat" film. Like the article, the film is just the story of us. It is a picture of how we choose to live our lives. In both the article and the film, Steve and I were careful to never say that because we live a certain way, others should live that way, as well. We are always taken aback when someone hits the "dislike" button on the YouTube film. *Really?* How do you dislike someone's personal testimony? Our son, Stephen, in particular, takes every "dislike" very personally. He doesn't understand how someone can dislike the film and assumes that a dislike means that they don't like his dad. We're helping him learn to just let those little hurts go and to focus, instead, on the thousands of "likes" that the film has received, as well as the positive comments left by well-wishers.

The film has some hot spots that have caused people to evaluate their own lives and the choices they are making. The article had hot spots, as well. One topic, in particular, really stirred up controversy with some of our friends. In the article, Margaret quoted me as saying that our children didn't participate in sports because I thought that sports were "unChristlike." We've never really been sure where she came up with that quote. We did discuss sports, but remember, I was an athlete and sports had always been a part of my life.

What we did discuss with Margaret was the over-emphasis, by parents, on winning and on sports as a priority. That very month had seen the murder of an ice hockey coach by a father, incensed by his son's lack of playing time. In our area, sports for our children were not possible because every sport had Sunday games or meets. We were committed to church as our priority and concerned by the willingness of Christian parents to acquiesce to the new Sunday sports paradigm. Really, that was the extent of our sports discussion.

We soon found out just how powerful the media and the written word would be to our friends. Regardless of our explanation of Margaret's quote, they were offended. How could we say that sports were un-Christlike? (*Umm, we didn't.*) They saw it in print and, therefore, it must be true. *Wow!* What an eye-opener for us and again, another opportunity to teach our children how to discern what is truth and what is simply ear-tickling error. We could only surmise that somehow the sport quote had hit a "hot spot" with our friends and they weren't comfortable scrutinizing their choices in that area.

Fifteen-Minutes of Fame

While the *New York Times* received letters to the editor, we began to receive phone calls. Michael Farris, the original subject of the article, was one of the first people to contact us. Although we had no idea what was coming, he sensed that we were about to be inundated with requests. He lent us his press secretary and that dear man shielded our family from interviews and phone calls that would have done us nothing but harm. We did conduct several interviews by phone and we received mail and phone calls from many people who had been affected, one way or another, by the article. To this day, we still receive at least one contact a year, usually from a young person wanting to know if our family still believes the way that we did then. The answer is *yes*.

Two things about the article really surprised us. Many people who would not consider themselves to be Christians voiced strong support for our family and our beliefs. At the same time, many Christians felt threatened by our choices and reacted negatively to the article. For us, we couldn't really understand the interest in our family. We were just a normal family of nine trying to live out lives that demonstrated the character of Christ.

That article and what Steve called our "Fifteen minutes of fame," in a small way prepared us for what would come after the release of our son Peter's documentary film, "In My Seat." After the article, we were somewhat taken aback by people's response and by their desire to connect with us. After the film, we were ready to minister and respond to the people who would contact us; people who were touched and changed by God's message of substitutionary atonement, as portrayed by Peter, in the film. As always, God was faithfully preparing us for what would come next. We were beginning to realize that the next steps were coming faster and faster. But for now, the only next we knew for certain was that it was time to leave Pennsylvania and follow God to Maine.

Our church planting days had begun.

Chapter 7

The Master's Call

Steve finished his first Master's degree from Calvary Baptist Theological Seminary in May 2000, and we were off to Maine. Steve was bubbling over with ideas and excitement; plans to start a new church to the honor and glory of God. All of those years of training were about to be put to the test and our whole family was thrilled. We were confident that all of Steve's classroom work, combined with our years of experience in Young Life and other ministries, had prepared us for what was to come. I think that if we had known all that the next ten years would hold, we would have been as frightened as we were excited. Thankfully, God only shows us one step at a time.

Cornerstone Baptist Church opened its doors on July 9, 2000. That first Sunday, there were twenty-eight people in attendance and nine of them were Scheibners. Our "Charlie Brown" pulpit was a wooden music stand that Steve had painted the night before our first service. We were a small group, but we were excited. The folks gathered that first Sunday were eager to grow in their own relationships with the Lord and to have an impact on the local community. Steve was eager to preach and teach. The church was off to a great start.

Building on the Cornerstone

In the beginning, we met in a local grange. For those outside of New England, a grange is a foreign concept, but here in Maine, the grange was once the hub of the community. Today, granges are standing vacant, except for the monthly Bean Supper, so we were able to rent the facility to use for the church. Yes, once a month, our Sunday morning services had the faint smell of New England baked beans, but we were happy to have a space that we could call home for Cornerstone. For four years that grange hosted church services, Awana clubs, ladies groups, and the all-important yearly Talent Show. Honestly, year after year, that talent show attracted people who would have never considered coming to a church service.

Steve was determined that from the start, Cornerstone would be a full-service church. So, small as we were, from day one the church had Sunday School, evening church, mid-week prayer service, children's outreach, women's Bible study, men's discipleship, and youth/parent teaching. Quite an ambitious start and Steve was totally involved with every aspect of the ministry. Steve envisioned a family-oriented church with strong male leaders, and so he taught and led with that vision at the forefront of his mind.

Soon, people began to hear that something new and exciting was going on in the community. We quickly moved from twenty-eight people to fifty and then one hundred, and more. I remember our first visitors. Steve and I were sitting on the grange steps before our first evening service. A car pulled into the parking lot and two people emerged. I excitedly said to Steve, "Look, its our first visitors!" His response, "Nah, they're probably just parking here to go to the Dairy Queen." When we saw the Bibles in their hands it was confirmed, Cornerstone had some brand new attendees!

Those early days at the church were exciting times. People were so eager to grow and be actively involved in ministry to others. Being in a military town, the church benefited from the military families who arrived at the church ready to serve. Steve was, and is, a great teacher and the congregation thrived under his teaching. Sadly, those exciting days couldn't last forever. Within a few years, sin and moral failure robbed Cornerstone of much of the innocence and joy of those first days.

God had prepared Steve to pastor Cornerstone. As he walked individuals and couples through difficult times of moral failure, and as he equipped the church to deal with trust-robbing behaviors among the leadership, Steve helped the church to remain unified and cohesive. Under his leadership, the church embraced those who had fallen and ministered to their bruised and hurting families. For Steve, however, the burden of such heavy counseling and carrying the load of normal pastoral responsibilities began to take its toll. As those in leadership were forced to step down from their positions because of unbiblical decisions, Steve found himself responsible for more and more of the church duties.

If you asked Steve, he would tell you that pastoring a church in New England was the hardest job he ever undertook. If you talked to me, being married to Steve while he pastored a church in New England was the most challenging time in our lives. If you listened to our children … I think you get the picture. Our whole family was totally committed to the church, and when the church was hurting, our family was in pain as well.

Those ten years of church planting were a time of stark contrasts. We experienced the joy and excitement of new believers and the hurt of misunderstanding and judgment. We rejoiced with couples and families as they made new commitments to one another and sorrowed with families that broke apart or just gave up. We had great times of laughter and equally painful times of tears. People grew and reveled in the Word of God, while at other times issues in the body threatened to tear the church apart.

A pastor's life is a manic life at times. Steve would go from counseling couples to praying over a newborn to unclogging church toilets to teaching a men's group. Emotionally, this was a new experience for him. He has always said that God was using the church to help us to develop a thicker skin, but at times, I'm not so sure. For me, until we became a pastor's family and experienced life under the magnifying glass, I couldn't have imagined the pain and isolation that sometimes comes with the territory. The lessons that we were learning hadn't been taught at seminary, they needed to be experienced in order to be understood.

At the same time that Steve was working hard to pastor the church effectively, God was working His plan to develop what would come next in our lives. The church would become just one strand in a three-strand cord that God would use to grow us up and to hone and sharpen our ministry focus.

God's Call to Character

In October of 2001, shortly after the hijackings of September 11th, Steve was tasked to write a course for the Navy. As a reservist, attached to the Active Duty Commodore's staff, Steve's job was to carry out special projects for the Commodore. One day, when he went to the Commodore to procure his next assignment, the Commodore set him on a path that would change his life direction and our ministry direction permanently. Of course, we didn't realize that at the time, but as always, God was working His plans behind the scenes.

When Steve went into the Commodore's office that day, he observed two, somewhat miserable looking, sailors leaving the office. Upon sitting down across from his superior, he noticed that the Commodore didn't look much better. When Steve questioned him about what was wrong, the Commodore shared the struggle he was facing.

The two sailors, a male and a female, were married to each other and they had a young child. The previous Christmas season, when the child was just nine months old, that young couple had decided to go shopping and then see a movie. However, instead of hiring a babysitter, they just left their baby home alone, in a crib. Of course, the baby soon began crying. The neighbors heard the crying and knocked on the door … no answer. Concerned, the neighbors next called the police, who called the fire department, who broke into the home. Fortunately, the baby was fine, but when the young couple returned, the police were waiting to greet them.

It was this young couple's response to what had transpired that was causing the Commodore to look so distressed. For months, the couple had been moving through a very elaborate military discipline system and from the night of the incident to that very afternoon in the Commodore's office, their response had remained stubbornly obstinate. All along, their only reaction to their irresponsibility had been this, "Hey, everyone else is doing it. Why are you coming down so hard on us?" They just wouldn't accept that they had done anything wrong.

Regardless of whether others were doing it or not, the couple's complete refusal to accept responsibility had tied the Commodore's hands; he had no choice but to discharge them from the Navy. That afternoon in his office he peppered Steve with the same type of question, over and over. "Why would they leave their child?" "Why wouldn't they admit that they were wrong?" "Why would they rationalize their behavior?" "Why, why, why?"

Steve's response to the Commodore that day would set in motion the foundation for today's Characterhealth ministry. He told the Commodore this, "You are asking the wrong question. You're asking, why? Today's sailors are asking, Why Not." He went on to explain the difference in the questions to the Commodore. He explained that the "Why not" generation is only interested in whether or not they will get in trouble for their choices. If it feels good, looks enjoyable, or if everyone else is doing it, then, why not? The Commodore was dealing with a generation that elevated the feeling of the moment over any established virtue or character quality. Their lack of inner character or core values inhibited them from making wise decisions.

The Commodore got it. That afternoon he gave Steve his next assignment, one that would become his permanent assignment for the rest of his career in the Navy. He tasked Steve to write a course that would teach the desperately needed character qualities that these young sailors lacked. In essence, he wanted Steve to teach morality to a group of young people who had never learned to make moral choices. Steve had his mission.

Divine Impact

At first, the class was taught to troublemakers. Getting ordered to go to the Navy Core Values class was perceived as punishment. However, soon the word began to spread. Course critiques came back to the Commanding Officers filled out, front and back. The comments went along the lines of: "Life changing, make the class longer, best teaching I've ever had, send me back again." Soon, Steve was teaching whole squadrons and specialty groups of Master Chiefs and Senior Officers. Not only were sailors enjoying the class, but also, squadrons were seeing increased productivity and lessened discipline issues. These young sailors, and some not-so-young sailors, were hungry for teaching about how to lead a character driven life. They asked if Steve could teach the course to their wives and children. Suddenly, Steve was traveling overseas and across the country to teach the course, ultimately reaching ten-thousand sailors.

That Navy course was strand number two. Strand number one was the church and soon, God would show us the third strand of the cord that would tie together our future ministry.

Even when we were living in Pennsylvania, Steve and I had taught parenting classes out of our home. Although we had used various teaching programs, more and more we were developing our own material, as we saw and recognized new needs in the parenting community. Old established assumptions about what parents already knew were being discarded as we realized that more and more young parents were coming into the parenting process ill-equipped to make wise parenting decisions. These young parents were seeking to learn how to live character-healthy lives themselves and until they accomplished that, they were unprepared to teach their children how to live biblically.

Just like the young sailors that Steve was teaching, we were realizing that a majority of the young parents in our classes had no idea how to live out or teach character to their children. Many of these parents weren't sure what good character looked like in their own lives and so they found themselves unable to pass on what they didn't possess. Virtuous decision-making that had been the accepted norm thirty years ago had given way to a feelings-driven culture and therefore, a "feelings-driven" parenting process.

Soon, the Navy Core Values class and the Parenting Matters classes began to look very similar. Lessons like: Choosing Pro-Activity over Re-Activity, Learning to Elevate Virtues Above Feelings, and the Decision-Depot Model, struck a chord with parents, sailors, and importantly, young people. Just like the sailors in Steve's Navy classes, the young couples soaked in the teaching and wanted more. Steve began teaching the basic lessons to high school students and they, too, embraced the concepts. Character healthy living, as found in the books of Romans and II Peter, was becoming the focus of our teaching.

It seemed like everywhere we turned, we saw the need for Christlike character training. At home, we spent hours teaching our own children. As well, we opened our home to a young single mother and her two children. She became a part of our family and we quickly saw her make changes for the good in her life as she embraced a biblical and character-healthy lifestyle. Suddenly, she was evaluating what was at stake in her decision making process, something she had never been encouraged to do, before. We wondered how many other young, single mothers found themselves in her position simply because they had never been taught to elevate virtues over feelings.

As families in the church spent time investing in character training, visitors to the church began to comment on the difference they saw in the young adults and children. The difference wasn't an outward look but instead, was a culture of excellence and Christ-like character. God was receiving the glory through the lives of these character-healthy families. God was beginning the process of showing Steve where He wanted us to go.

Whenever it has been time to make important decisions in our life, Steve and I have watched God begin the push and pull process. There are times that all of us feel the push to leave something. "It's too hard." "It's no fun anymore." "I'm tired of this…" The push can be strong but it isn't necessarily God's will. Other times the pull of life takes over. "I'd love to do that!" "That looks more interesting!" "They really need me…" Again, even a strong pull isn't enough to simply yank up our stakes and move on. However, when the push and pull are happening at the same time, we believe it is God prompting and directing a change.

Divine Leading

For Steve, the push to step away from the church began about five years into his ministry at Cornerstone. In the first few years, Steve had begun each day excited to get up and go to work at the church. However, when the heavy counseling and moral failures amongst the church's leadership began to pile up, he began to experience what we called, "Dark Days." I had never seen Steve less than upbeat and optimistic and those days were hard to endure. As the stress increased, the dark days became full-on depression and our family watched as Steve would come home just to sit and stare. He could pull it together to fulfill his public ministry and other responsibilities, but the effort would totally drain him and he had nothing left to give. We couldn't help him and the children and I began to feel helpless and hopeless.

At the same time, God was keeping Steve's inner excitement alive with the development of the character teaching. He loved to see young people and families changed by the biblical teaching and the practical applications we offered. Those moments of breaking through someone's old and established paradigms in order to introduce them to character-healthy living kept Steve going. For him, life became a series of bearable highs and steep, stark, really unbearable lows.

God was introducing the push and the pull, but we needed space to step back and recognize His hand. In the spring of 2009, Steve's depression symptoms had become more pronounced. He was gaining weight, suffering short-term memory loss, and dealing with increasingly sharp chest pains. He told the deacons that he needed a six-month sabbatical and they graciously said yes. That decision was made in February and Steve's sabbatical began in May. We weren't sure he could make it that long as we watched him become more and more desperate for a break from the ongoing pressure of his daily responsibilities.

I wish I could say that sabbatical was a cure-all. It wasn't, but it gave Steve some much-needed breathing space and allowed us time to pray and seek God's face. Steve had told the church for years that he would retire as their pastor and leaving Cornerstone just didn't seem like an option. We hoped that perhaps he just needed a break from the heavy-duty counseling and daily stress. Steve spent the summer resting, playing with the children, and working on his Doctoral thesis. Slowly, his smile came back and he was enjoying life again. However, he was still fragile and seemingly small discouragements sent him back to a dark place. Still, we were beginning to see glimpses of the old, positive Steve.

We ended the sabbatical with a mission trip to South Africa. While there, we taught our Parenting Matters course to forty-five parents and we were thrilled to see them embrace the teaching just as eagerly as their American counterparts. Around the world, parents were hungry to learn how to instill Godly character into their children's lives. God was showing us something, but we still weren't prepared to see it clearly. While we were in South Africa, our friend Dave Rudolph took us out for a drive and while he had us in the car asked permission to share his thoughts about our ministry.

He told us that he felt like God was calling Steve out of the pastorate and into fulltime ministry to families. Dave is an over-the-top-idea guy, just like Steve, so although we thanked him for his insights, we didn't necessarily agree. We still felt obligated to minister at Cornerstone, the pull away just wasn't clear to us.

Zigzagging in the Right Direction

We returned home from the sabbatical rested and prayed up. We both agreed that we could stay at the church, that all Steve had needed was some time off. Boy, were we ever wrong! Within one week of being back to his position of Senior Pastor, Steve sunk into the worst depression he had faced up to that point. Nothing particularly bad had happened, just the usual day-to-day ups and downs of church ministry, but again, he was in rough shape. God had gotten his attention and was demanding his obedience. It was obvious that it was time to step away from Cornerstone and move on into our next phase of ministry.

Once the decision was made, Steve was almost giddy. He wanted to step down right then and there and get on to the next thing. However, our children had grown up, for the most part, at Cornerstone and we felt like we needed to seek their input on our decision, as well. A few weeks later, when our college children were home on break, we called a family conference. Steve told the children what God had laid on his heart and that he felt that he needed to step down from the church in order to follow God in obedience. Not surprisingly, God had been preparing our children's hearts, too. Although they loved the church, to a child, they were eager to follow God's leading. The six months of having their positive, not-depressed father back had shown them just how much the depression was affecting our family and they didn't want to go there again. We'd always worked hard to develop our family identity and Team Scheibner was united in pursuing this new adventure. It was a great time spiritually for our family as we rested in God's leading We knew we could trust Him for the final outcome of this decision.

For several years, folks had jokingly been saying that they were afraid that Steve would leave to start a parenting ministry. In the midst of the jokes, I think that God was preparing hearts. The Sunday that Steve announced his resignation there were so many people encouraging us in our new ministry direction. Of course, some people didn't, or wouldn't, or perhaps couldn't understand our decision, (coincidently, these are the same people who don't like ice-cream,) but Steve was so peaceful in God's will that their criticism couldn't undermine his determination to follow the Lord.

Steve announced his resignation in January and stepped down the last weekend in May. By that time, the church had called the Assistant Pastor to fill Steve's position. On May 29, 2010, Steve preached his last sermon at Cornerstone. His first one had been entitled, "Sometimes the Shortest Distance Between Two Points is a Zigzag." For ten years, God had taken Steve and our family on a zigzag path to show us clearly where He wanted us to be, now was the time to follow Him in faithful obedience.

Steve stepped down from the church on a Sunday and the very next day we launched the Characterhealth ministry. For ten years we had been developing the materials that would become our ministry's foundation. For ten years, God had been using the three strands of the church, the Navy, and the parenting ministry to increase our commitment, discernment, patience, mercy, long-suffering, steadfastness, and so much more. For five years, facing Steve's depression had taught all of us how to have more compassion and mercy toward others, especially other pastors. Now, our prayer was that we could come alongside those pastors and minister together to influence families and encourage them to train a new generation of courageous, Christlike, character-healthy leaders. The foundation was in place, now was the time to see what God would do.

Chapter 8

Christlike and Character Healthy

For years, Steve and I had been teaching Parenting Matters, Marriage Matters, and Character Matters conferences, now it was time for all of those ministries to come together into one cohesive whole. Much like the slow but steady process that God had employed to put oil into Steve's life, the building of the Characterhealth ministry would need to be a slow and steady oil filling process, as well.

First things first though, this new ministry needed a distinctive name that encapsulated all that we hoped to accomplish. As we searched for the right name to describe our ministry, Steve made an interesting discovery. In our teaching, we have always talked about our generations over-emphasis on physical well being. We have become a nation that is preoccupied with health and safety. From wet wipes at the grocery story door, to helmets and elbow pads for playground safety, we leave no stone unturned in the quest to keep our children physically safe. As well, for several generations, schools and professionals have stressed a focus on our emotional wellbeing. The self-esteem movement has spent time and money convincing us that if our children just felt better about themselves, they would be more successful and more secure. That experiment has been a monumental failure, as evidenced by ever-increasing drug use, promiscuity, and suicide, by the very children that we are told should feel the best about themselves. What about our children's character? We wondered if anyone was writing or speaking about the need for healthy character.

On a whim, Steve Googled the expression, *Character Health*, interested to see what he would discover. Although, we were surprised by his findings, we probably shouldn't have been. At that time, when you typed the words *Character* and *Health* into a search engine, the top findings were sites devoted to helping you increase the health of your video game character. The subject of virtue, or moral character, was totally missing. Today, when you type those same words, our ministry appears at the top of the page. If we can have any influence, it will be to convince this generation of the need for strong and biblically based character health.

Our name was born. We purchased the name Characterhealth and began the formation of the Characterhealth Corporation. While both Steve and I would agree that physical and emotional health are important components of a person's life, it is a person's character health that is of foremost importance and a lack of character healthy behavior will be detrimental to all other areas of life. With that in mind, we now set out to: Equip parents to raise the next generation of Christlike, character healthy leaders.

What Is Character Health?

It's what Christlikeness looks like in practice. Stated simply, *character health is the balance that characterizes Christlike believers as they consistently elevate virtues above feelings, when faced with a moral dilemma.* Character healthy people put God's Word first. Character health (Christlikeness) should be what we are seeking when we look for happiness or satisfaction. The reason that most of us do not live character healthy lives is because we are taught to approach character as a means to an end, rather than as a Biblically and morally satisfying end in its self.

We think of character health in the same way that you would think of physical or emotional health. You exercise to take care of your body, you read a good book or take a vacation to maintain your emotional health, but what do you do to strengthen the health of your character? Isn't character health important? Does it have any positive influence on our overall wellbeing? Steve and I contend that healthy character is essential to our overall health and that maintaining healthy character will bring Glory to God. As we allow God to add moral excellence, (*virtue*, 2 Peter 1:5) to our faith, it will benefit every aspect of our lives.

This understanding of the need for character-healthy living became our mission, and Steve and I committed to spending our lives training up and capturing the hearts of this next generation of young people so that they might grow up in character healthy homes, families, and communities. The ministries of Parenting Matters, Marriage Matters, and Character Matters became devoted to helping people learn the character healthy discipline of consistently elevating virtues above feelings. The aim of our ministry would be to seek God's glory by training up young and old alike to come to faith in Jesus Christ and grow daily in the character healthy pursuit of Christlikeness.

A Bridge to Godly Living

Our ministry to the Navy and to young couples over the past 10 years had shown us that people were hungry for this type of character-driven teaching. With the Navy folks, many had no foundation at all upon which to build a habit of character healthy decision-making. The sum total of their decision-making process rested in determining what everyone else was doing. In the church, we had found that the core of character was not much different than in the Navy world. Although we had many people who could recite verses or who read their bibles through faithfully every year, few could take the truths found in the scripture and apply those truths to everyday life.

The ministry of Characterhealth became a bridge, taking Bible truths and showing people how to make accurate biblical and character building applications out of those truths.

"What does it look like Tuesday afternoon?" became the tagline of our conferences. We wanted people to not simply have a head knowledge of the Word of God, but a strong grasp of how to live that knowledge out in a practical and daily way. Looking spiritual on the outside was never our goal; we wanted to help people develop hearts that loved God and desired to live lives that would be pleasing to Him.

We both would have loved to just take off and start teaching conferences and leading studies, but unfortunately, that's not how starting a ministry, begins. We were amazed at all of the paperwork and filing that was required to become a non-profit ministry. For my part, I was surprised by just how expensive it was to start a not-for-profit ministry. However, all that work was part of putting oil into the Characterhealth lamp and so work we did. Step by step, the Characterhealth ministry was developing a strong foundation.

Besides setting up the administrative side of the ministry, the first year was spent producing materials for our conferences. Steve and I had, by that time, written several books as well as the companion curriculums for our parenting, marriage, and character conferences. All of these materials would need to be bound and so bookbinding became the Scheibner family business. Nate and Baleigh spent days binding books, while Stephen collated them, and Taylor cut the bindings to the correct size. Characterhealth truly became a family ministry as we spent hours together laughing over the crunch of the bookbinding machines.

Several years earlier, Steve and I had filmed the Parenting Matters teaching. Steve's childhood buddy, Pete Shaner, was now a director in Los Angeles. He came in for a week and with the help of the church teens, filmed the ten-week series. Families who had previously been in our classes attended the filming to provide an audience and to ask live questions. Afterwards, our son, Peter, spent hours editing the finished product and preparing it to be duplicated.

After that filming, the teens were ready for more and bigger responsibility. Taking the skills they had learned from Pete, the teen boys filmed Steve teaching Character Matters to a group of young people. They did a phenomenal job and we were proud to be able to offer those finished DVDs at our conferences, as well as the "professionally" filmed Parenting Matters. For our son, Peter, this experience was of great value when he later started school as a filmmaker.

As the first year of the Characterhealth ministry continued, we continued to add more resources to assist people in their character growth process. We introduced the Characterhealth Character Quality of the Day, a short daily email with a highlighted character quality and an applicable parenting point to help parents make the character quality real, at home. People's response to this resource was overwhelmingly positive, but still there was a need for more.

Steve and I loved teaching conferences and we did several that first year. However, every time we left a conference, the attendees had the same complaint. They would always be disappointed by the fact that they couldn't have personal access to us. Nearly everyone wanted the freedom to email or call us with their daily questions or parenting dilemmas. Steve and I talked about filling this need, but we knew that it would be nearly impossible for us to parent our own children if we were inundated with hundreds of parenting questions. Still, we wanted to find a solution for these parents.

Out of that need was birthed the Parenting Matters bi-monthly conference calls. We began to offer folks who joined our ministry the opportunity to call in, twice a month, on a conference call where they could ask us their parenting questions, directly. What a blessing these calls have been. Many folks call in with questions and probably just as many call in just to listen and learn from other people. As needs were arising, God was faithfully showing us the way to meet those needs.

During that first year, I was busy writing books and bible studies for moms and student athletes. Steve was super busy as well. Besides still working for the airlines and running the day-to-day operations of the ministry, he was completing his Doctorate. The boy, who had grown up in a broken home, with two alcoholic fathers and a hands-off mother, wrote his doctoral dissertation on this topic: "The Role of Parents in the Character Development of Children." Only God could have brought about an outcome like that! Steve learned all that he needed to learn about parenting from the Word of God and he reflected that learning in his doctoral dissertation.

God provided us with a Board of Directors and friends who assisted and advised us along the way. Our website was designed and managed as a gift to the ministry. Our conference booklets were produced as a donation. A friend who was involved in another ministry "lent" us three workers to make calls about our ministry. Everything was falling into place and God's oil was beginning to fill the Characterhealth lamp.

All that was needed now was the spark that would ignite the oil of our ministry. Just like September 11, 2001, had provided that ignition in Steve's life, the 10th anniversary of the hijackings would provide the same type of spark that now has become a blazing flame. On August 31, 2011, our ability to minister rose to a whole new level with the release of our son's film, "In My Seat: A Pilot's Story."

Chapter 9

Making Our Marks ... *For the Kingdom*

On March 22, 1988, Peter Warren Scheibner entered the world, a month early and determined to be heard. With his birth, I was no longer Megan Scheibner; instead, I became "Peter's Mom." I have eight children now and they are all special, but none of the others evoked this response from people. Peter, from birth, was bound and determined to leave his mark on the world.

Peter, or P-2 as I call him, spent a large part of his childhood chafing at the constraints of being just a boy. He desperately wanted to be a leader and to have his ideas adopted and validated. I spent that childhood of his explaining over and over that he needed to earn the right to be heard and that his submission to authority as a child would earn him the respect he longed for as an adult. It was hard, but Peter eventually embraced the lesson and invested his teen and early college years learning to be a follower, so that someday he could be an effective leader.

Like his father, Peter is a total idea guy. Once, when Peter was about four years old, he looked up from the dinner table, stuck two fingers in the air, (ala Richard Nixon) and emphatically stated, "I have an idea!" The next moment he said this, "How about you buy some candy and a movie and I'll eat the candy and watch the movie." We laughed so hard and that night, he actually got the candy and the movie.

Sometimes, because Peter and Steve are so much alike, they have found themselves at odds and when Peter was young, his relationship with his dad was often strained. Since Peter is like a young Steve, he and I have always been extraordinarily close. In fact, as I was writing this book, every time I talked to Peter he would regale me with, "You can't forget to say this ..." (He's full of ideas!) Peter embraces life and everything he puts his hand to with gusto. If something needs to get done, Peter is your guy.

Peter, himself, would tell you that it hasn't always been that way. In our Parenting Matters course we talk about the correct order of responsibilities for our kids. We strongly believe that our children need to learn to be faithful at home and in the family context before they gain recognition outside of the home. Many of the principles we teach in that lesson have been developed as we parented Peter. Peter was the boy that every adult turned to for help. He was mature beyond his years and well spoken. Outside of our home, he was in great demand as a children's worker, sound room technician, and set-up guy. However, inside our home was a different story

Battles With a Strong-Will

At home, we continually battled Peter to keep his room clean, to maintain his school log, and to complete his chores. The public and the private persona just weren't matching up and we knew that until he learned to be faithful at home, God wouldn't allow him to be a true leader outside the home. As well, not learning those lessons of faithfulness and carefulness at home would make him an undependable husband and father someday. Daily, we tried to live out Galatians 6:9: "Let us not become weary in doing good, for at the proper time we will reap a harvest if we do not give up." We knew that once Peter was out on his own, our influence would become limited, at best, so we wanted to do our best to instill that faithful character.

Sometimes, parenting isn't pleasant and in fact, it can be downright painful. However, we loved Peter and we were committed to doing whatever it took to help him learn the lessons of faithfulness that were lacking in his character. After his freshman year of college, Peter came home for the summer. He had been promoted to the position of manager at our local Target store, the youngest manager in any Target nationwide. He was doing a great job and his employers were rewarding him with praise and incentives. That public persona was firmly intact, but still, the home front wasn't looking good.

That May, our family left on our annual two-week vacation. Because of his job, Peter remained at home. When we left, Steve told Peter that his only responsibility was to make sure that the lawn was mowed. While we were gone, Steve reminded Peter several times and Peter told us that it was, "No problem." We believed him.

We returned home to Maine just as the sun was setting. As we pulled up the driveway, everyone in the car fell silent as we observed the knee-high grass. The younger Scheiblets scattered as Steve walked into the house to be greeted enthusiastically by Peter. When Steve asked what happened to the lawn, Peter's countenance fell and then he stammered out that the lawn mower was broken. Steve marched out to the garage, ripped that lawn mower cord, and when the engine roared to life he mowed our entire lawn, in the dark. That time in the dark helped him to work off some anger but he sure did a rotten job on the lawn! The time mowing in the dark gave Steve time to pray and consider what needed to happen next.

When Steve came back into the house, he was ready to deliver a lesson that would change Peter and the characterization of Peter's life, forever. Because we co-signed Peter's college loans, he was dependent on us to go back to school. Steve explained to Peter that we couldn't afford to pay back his loans and because he was characterized by unfaithfulness in his responsibilities, we couldn't take a chance on co-signing another loan. He told Peter that we would support him returning to college, we just wouldn't help to pay for it.

What a low moment for both Steve and Peter. Steve was angry, Peter was angry; it was a long summer. I can't tell you how many times that summer Steve wanted to relent and sign the loans, but he didn't. Peter's character was too important to us and we had to be willing to make a hard stand. We realized that our days of influence in his life were becoming numbered and we needed to impart this lesson. Steve and Peter lived an uneasy truce for many months.

Peter stayed home that entire year. He worked at Target and put away some money. More importantly, his attitude toward his home responsibilities changed; they became as important as his public responsibilities. Steve and Peter slowly began to rebuild their relationship.

The next year, Peter returned to school. About two months into the school year, he called his father. He told Steve that he just wanted to thank him. Steve asked why he was thanking him. Peter explained that now that he had returned to school, he was watching the kids whose parents were paying their way, kids with no responsibilities, and he was realizing how immature and ungrateful they were. Peter said these words to his dad, "Thank you, Dad. I got the lesson. I know it was hard for you, but it was the right thing to do." A moment like that can't be bought; it's priceless. That moment started a new chapter in Steve and Peter's relationship, a new chapter that is flourishing today.

Peter was right. He did get the lesson and since then, he has been a young man of impeccable character and faithfulness. His testimony has been his protection on more than one occasion. Steve and Peter have a wonderful relationship, now. Steve considers Peter to be one of his closest friends and more importantly, he trusts him implicitly. God used Steve to teach Peter the hard lesson of faithfulness in his character and that lesson is still bearing great fruit today.

From Boy to Godly Man

Peter returned to school determined to continue building the reputation he would need if he ever wanted to earn the right to be heard. Peter is named after Steve's childhood friend, Pete Shaner, and like Pete, he decided to become a filmmaker. The love of filmmaking has always been in Peter's DNA. As a teenager, he wrote and filmed many movies with his friends and with his younger siblings. In fact, one year we had the Scheibner Family Academy awards, complete with gowns and suits, and it was there that Peter won his first Best Director award. Peter spent so many hours editing the Parenting Matters series that he has large sections memorized. As well, he edits and uploads our Characterhealth Character Points on Youtube. He is good at what he does and just as importantly; he loves doing it.

Soon, it was time for Peter to begin his senior film project. By this time, Peter was twenty-two and in love. He was engaged to his college sweetheart, Rochelle, and romance was on his mind. He wrote and turned in a preliminary script to his professors, laying out a sweet love story. To his chagrin, they turned down his proposal. When Peter later met with the committee, they told him that the only project they would accept from him would be a project about his dad's 9/11 story. The committee knew that Steve had a powerful story to tell and they realized that no one could tell it better than his son. They were adamant and Peter had no choice but to agree to their film proposal.

Here's the honest truth. Peter did not want to film a 9/11 documentary. Steve's story had been part of our family for nine years at that point and it was an emotional and troubling story for our kids. We had begun leaving the children home whenever Steve was sharing his story in another pulpit; the graphic images that developed in their minds of Tom dying in Steve's place were just too heavy a load for the children to carry, over and over again. Nevertheless, Peter began the filming process and once he got going, the idea guy inside of him began to ferment and create.

An Eye on Eternity

In February, Steve and I met Peter and his new bride in New York City to do some filming. We spent the day visiting the reconstruction site of the World Trade Centers and taking any footage that Peter thought would be useful. Toward the end of the day, we passed the metal cross outside Ground Zero. The rest of us kept walking, but Peter ran back to film the cross and that photo became a powerful element of the film. Peter just has an eye for what makes a good film, and God has uniquely suited him for what he does.

Even with the ideas flowing, the film was not an easy project for Peter to complete. As he spent weeks working through the Betty Ong portion of the film, he began to have "Dark Days," much like his father had experienced. Our whole family prayed Peter through that film and his sweet wife provided the listening ear he needed to talk through all the emotions that he was processing. At one point, Peter hit an impasse and just couldn't get the film completed. One of his professors listened for an hour and then spent another hour asking Peter probing questions. That pivotal time boosted Peter over his mental block and suddenly, the film all came together.

August brought Peter home for his sister's wedding. At that time, he showed us some of the preliminary footage and Steve knew immediately that Peter had created something very special and very powerful. He urged Peter to speed up production for a 9/11-anniversary release. Despite unnecessary delays from the University committee and many unforeseen hurdles, the film was released to YouTube on August 31st.

To say that we were unprepared for the release would be a huge understatement. We had no advertising planned. We had no distribution system in place. Suddenly, we were getting inundated with phone calls and emails from pastors who wanted to use the film in their 9/11 church services. Team Scheibner went to work again. Our two youngest boys spent hours duplicating and labeling the DVDs. For days, we made multiple trips to the Post Office to mail off stacks of DVDs. Steve was speaking in Greenville, SC, on the anniversary of 9/11 and as we made the 18 hour drive south, we found ourselves forced to pull over every couple hours to mail more copies of the film. I think we know the location of every FedEx store between Maine and South Carolina!

Interview requests began to come in, both from here in the United States and from as far away as Belfast, Ireland. We couldn't keep up with the emails that were flooding our inbox. People were writing to tell us that their lives were profoundly impacted from watching the film. They were passing the film on to all of their friends, who in turn passed the film along even further. We watched the views on Youtube multiply by the hour. Peter started to receive emails from all over the world. We found ourselves touched by the comments posted on the film's Youtube wall and we were humbled by comments like these:

You are an amazing individual with an amazing story. I am deploying to Afghanistan in just days on this 10th anniversary. I will bring your story with me, and I hope it will change lives the same way it changed mine. I will carry an American flag with me everywhere I go in your honor, and I hope you will accept it when I return. You are a great American, and I assure you when it is your time, God will greet you with open arms saying "Well done, my good and faithful servant"

I am sitting here with tears in my eyes. Oh, how good to know the Lord and know that He is in charge of all things. What a story! What a blessing to know that this family was walking with the Lord, and to hear their testimony. God bless them and use them for His glory. And may those of us who know the Lord make good use of the time we have left. He could take us any time.

Perhaps, the most emotional e-mails and comments we received were from war veterans. Whether they were veterans of Vietnam, Korea, or the current war in Afghanistan, their remarks were eerily similar. These men and women shared the sorrow and guilt they suffered, knowing that they were alive, while fellow soldiers and sailors were dead. Many shared stories of friends stepping on land mines right in front of their eyes. All of those dear veterans thanked us for the film, explaining how it had helped with their guilt and how they felt hope for healing from the memories. I couldn't read their comments without tearing up.

A Picture of "Substitutionary Atonement"

God was doing something amazing! All we could do was sit back, watch, and marvel. On the morning of September 11, 2011, the Youtube video hit one-hundred thousand. We were thrilled. Honestly though, we all thought the interest in the film would drop off after the anniversary of September 11th had passed. Boy, were we wrong! It's been fourteen weeks now since the film's release and as of today, it is over 1.6 million views. The number of people seeing it for the first time grows daily.

This is what we've learned about the film. "In My Seat" isn't so much a story about 9/11. Instead, it is a story about substitutionary atonement. In Steve's story, people can clearly see and understand what it meant to have Christ die in their place. The old-time story of the gospel has found a modern-day application in film. Each and every time that Steve shares the film and his follow-on testimony, he has the joy of seeing people make new commitments to a relationship with Christ. Pastors write us every week to share that they are seeing the same results in their churches. God is at work and He is awakening a people to Himself.

For Peter, releasing the film was a mixed blessing. Whenever God does something big, there are always people who want to shoot the messenger. Peter was no exception and he was blindsided by some painful wounds. Thankfully, instead of becoming bitter, he has learned, through the film's release, to allow God to be his defender and because he worked so hard to develop his own faithful character, God has been faithful to encourage and uphold him. Those hard lessons at home have paid off in sweet fruit, now.

As a mom, whenever someone was particularly kind to my children, I would feel a special fondness for that person. As I have watched God protect, nurture, encourage, and lavish blessings on Peter, during this time, I find myself even more in love with my Lord than I was before. God is so good!

Both Steve and I are so proud of Peter. Proud of his work on the film, yes, but even more proud of his willingness to endure personal attacks in order to see the film released. God has used emails from persecuted Christians around the world to remind Peter of what is truly important-obedience and faithfulness to God, alone. The release of "In My Seat" has helped to develop spiritual muscle that will serve Peter well in the years to come.

"In My Seat" will begin a season of film competitions, soon. We're excited to see what happens in those competitions, but we are even more excited to see how God will reach people through their interaction with the film.

Characterhealth is a family ministry. Our youngest four serve at home. Our daughters have worked our book tables and promoted our literature. Now, Peter's film has provided the spark, the ignition that has lit the flame under the Characterhealth ministry. Our year of preparations is over and God is taking us places and building ministry partnerships that we never could have envisioned.

Peter has always wanted to make his mark on the world. At the age of twenty-three, he has done just that. "In My Seat" will be used as a tool for the Kingdom of God for the rest of Peter's life. His hard work paid off; he's earned the right to be heard.

And that's something, I'm thrilled to say, my whole family is learning. Let's jump back to what we believe is making the difference: *the home-schooling advantage.*

Chapter 10

The Home-Schooling Advantage

It was 1992, and Katie's first year of Kindergarten came very quickly for our family. Since the time that Katie was a baby, Steve and I had discussed just how our children would be educated. I had grown up in the Public schools and had great memories of my time there. However, for most of my schooling, I had been in the Accelerated Program and therefore, had not been forced to sit through classes. Instead, I was given my year's curriculum and set loose to complete the work on my own, only utilizing the teachers as a resource, or if I ran into problems. I loved this type of learning, although because there was so little supervision, I often got into trouble by pulling pranks with the two boys that were in the program with me.

Steve, on the other hand, had hated his Public school experience. Sitting in classrooms and waiting for the dismissal bell, long after he had finished his assigned work, had been a total frustration to him. Knowing that there was no incentive to get his work done early, had taught him to procrastinate and to simply get by with the bare minimum. He didn't want our children to experience the same thing.

Just as we took our parenting and character-building responsibilities seriously, we knew that our children's education was ultimately our responsibility, as well. We wondered how we would continue to be intimately involved in training our children if they were gone for the majority of the day. We loved observing the way that the children functioned together, as a team, and we weren't sure how the Public school would affect that dynamic.

We began to pray about the option of home education. We knew that I was capable of educating our children, but we wanted to make a wise decision. Some of our hesitation came from observing the homeschoolers that we knew. Too many of them seemed to change their educational philosophies monthly, or in some cases, weekly. We watched as their children went from home school, to private school, to public school, and finally, back home. For some, this transition happened all in one year. My children weren't old enough for school yet, but I knew that such extreme variations in educational systems couldn't be good for any child.

Sometimes, the home schooled teenagers that Steve and I worked with in the youth group talked about doing their schoolwork while wearing their pajamas all day. Again, this approach to education just didn't seem right to us, so early on, our opinion of home schooling was very mixed. We recognized that some of the brightest, most articulate children that we knew were home schooled, but we also knew some precocious, demanding children that were home schooled, as well. We determined to make our decision based solely on the Word of God and prayer, without considering how anyone else conducted their home schooling. Regardless of what anyone else was doing, or how they were doing it, we wanted to make the choice that was right for our family.

Cheerleaders and Naysayers

Our own families had mixed opinions about home schooling, as well. My mother had been a public school teacher and had written the reading curriculum used in her school district. We assumed that she would be opposed to us opting out of the public school system. Instead, she was our biggest cheerleader. She had always wished that she could have kept me home and she especially thought that home schooling would have been a better option for my brother, Tuck. Steve's mom wasn't as encouraging. She regarded with suspicion, anything that went against the norm of society. In fact, she was vocally opposed to our home schooling until she saw a show about home schooling on "Oprah." Wow! What a change in opinion! Suddenly, she couldn't wait to tell her friends about how dedicated we were as parents because we were choosing to home school, and how brilliant her grandchildren would be after we completed their education.

We prayed, and I researched and we planned and prepared. Then, we prayed and prepared some more. Finally, we determined that home schooling would be the choice for the Scheibner family. In 1992, it was time to put that decision to the test. Katie turned five and… we enrolled her in school. Even now, I'm not sure why we flinched and made that decision. I think some of the decision came from sheer exhaustion. We had just moved to Pennsylvania and given birth to Molly and I was just *TIRED!* I rationalized the decision by saying that Katie really needed to make friends in this new town and school would be the way to accomplish that goal.

It didn't take long for us to realize that we had made a mistake. The concern we had felt about damage to the family dynamic quickly became a reality. Katie began coming home from school and referring to her siblings as "those kids." The brother and sisters, who had been her best friends, suddenly became nothing more than an annoyance.

Besides the disruption to our family relationships, time spent investing in Katie's character became difficult to find. She came home from school exhausted and would often fall asleep for a couple hours. By the time she woke up, it was time to assist her with her homework, make dinner, take baths, and head to bed; only to get up, get on the bus, and do it all again.

I know that many families thrive on this type of school-day lifestyle, but for our family, it just wasn't working. An added negative was the attendance requirement. Steve had this wonderful job with the airline and we could fly for free. We planned educational and fun family trips, but soon the school called to say that Katie couldn't accompany us, because she would miss too many days of Kindergarten. Family building times versus Kindergarten attendance, it just didn't seem like a fair trade off to us. We realized that home schooling was the only option that would allow us the flexibility to travel with our kids and to take advantage of the opportunities that Steve's job brought to our family. As an added bonus, we would be able to plan our school schedule around Steve's flying schedule, allowing the children extra time with their dad when he was at home.

We finished out the school year with Katie, but we determined that from September forward, we would be a home schooling family. Once we made the final decision, it was never a year-to-year question for us. We felt confident of God's leading and we were equally confident that He could pull us out of home schooling if that ever became His desire.

Teaching Them to Stand Strong

From the beginning of our home-schooling adventure, we wanted to make sure that our primary focus wasn't simply academically superior children. Instead, we prayerfully established the three branches of our home schooling curriculum. Those three branches were Character-Building, Service to Others, and Challenging Academics.

The primary focus of our child training had always been character development. We wanted, more than any other goal, to equip our children to live Christlike, character-healthy lives. We determined that home schooling would be a part of that training, not a separate part of their lives, segregated from the daily character emphasis. Home schooling afforded us so many opportunities to teach character! Learning to be diligent and careful in their schoolwork took character. Learning to prioritize and stay focused on a project until it was completed took character. Learning to concentrate and not be silly with a sibling during school time took character. The opportunities for character growth multiplied every day.

The second, and equally important, branch of our home schooling was service to others. It was hard enough not to be child-centered in our parenting, being a home schooling parent made the opportunities for child-centeredness even more tempting. It was so easy to get sucked into the trap of spending all of my time, energy, and resources on making sure that my children were home schooled well. It was tempting to spend all of my free time reading home schooling magazines and evaluating home school supplies. I had to fight the urge to spend every moment and every conversation focused on the children and their never-ending needs. Steve and I both knew teens that had been the focus of their parents' every thought and we felt sorry for those kids. As they got older and realized that they weren't the center of the world, for some it was a difficult transition and a very rude awakening. We certainly didn't want that type of outcome for our children.

Along with the temptation to be child-centered, home schooling beckoned us to another unbiblical paradigm. We observed more and more home schooling families falling into a totally family-centered lifestyle.

Everything became about the family and making sure that your own family was satisfied and successful, at all costs. At the same time we were beginning to home school, many publications were touting the virtues of family-centeredness. We both believed that the family was God's primary tool to reach the world for Christ, but we just didn't agree that a total focus on the family, to the exclusion of others, was biblical. We were seeing families step over the line from concern for their families, to worship of their families. We wanted our family to be a light and a ministry to others, not just a self-centered destination in itself.

Service to others became our antidote to child/family-centeredness. We clearly saw that when we were intentionally finding ways to serve people outside our family, we all were more others-oriented and less self-focused. Because homeschooling did not confine us to an 8-2:30 schedule, it was easy to find opportunities to serve others. At various times, we cleaned the church nursery and sanctuary, prepared and delivered meals to folks in need, offered child-care, and enjoyed so many other opportunities. One of our favorite, and most-long term services, occurred at a camp my children attended. This camp was a year-round camp, but once the summer staff was gone and the camp was only used on weekends, the camp caretaker and his wife had to clean all of the bathrooms. This was a large camp and the task looked daunting. We discussed the need, as a family, and began to drive an hour every Monday morning to clean those bathrooms. What a great opportunity for service and what a great chance for my children to learn diligence and carefulness, in their work.

Every Monday, we scrubbed sinks, wiped down showers, and disinfected toilet bowls. Imagine my nine-year-olds surprise when she realized that the six "drinking fountains," that she cleaned each week, weren't actually drinking fountains, at all! My kids really developed an eye for making those bathrooms look nice and the caretaker and his wife were thrilled with the help they received. The hour-long car ride became a special time of laughter and Veggie-tale sing-alongs for the children and me, and a great way to start our week. We noticed a direct correlation between the amounts of time we spent serving and the amount of time spent bickering among our children. Positive family-time spent serving helped to unite the kids, while time spent "hanging out," or fulfilling their own desires, caused them to argue and focus on themselves. Besides the great lessons of being others-oriented, serving taught our children character qualities like: compassion, mercy, persistence, reliability, and so much more. Knowing that Steve and I considered service to be just as important a priority as actual bookwork helped our children to keep academics in its proper place.

Occasionally, we had well-meaning friends question us about the appropriateness of taking time off from doing bookwork in order to serve others. We always told them the same thing. Schools spend time and resources trying to manufacture situations to teach "about" service to their students. In our family home school, we could take the head-knowledge of service and put it into practice. The children learned more by filling actual needs than they ever could have learned by reading about or simulating service activities.

The third branch of our home schooling curriculum was challenging academics. In no way did we want our children to see home schooling as the easy alternative to Public school. One of my strengths had always been research, so I put that strength to work in choosing my children's curriculum. The first year we home schooled, I chose a packaged curriculum because I was afraid that to do otherwise would leave gaps in Katie's education. Very soon, I realized that the dreaded gaps were no concern at all. As we studied diligently, regardless of the curriculum, the gaps would take care of themselves.

From then on, instead of merely using packaged curricula, I began to observe how each of my children learned and then I custom-designed a different curriculum for each of them. Although there were certain books that I used with all of the children, in many areas, they used individual curriculums that were more appropriate to their interests and learning-styles. Often, Steve would point out an area that seemed to be frustrating one of the children, and together, we would decide whether the problem was the student's or the curriculum's.

If our curriculum became the problem, we were willing to change horses in midstream, but we tried to avoid that dynamic. We both realized that there were great lessons to be learned from staying with a less-than perfect teaching material. We wanted our children to realize that there were times in life that you just had to stick with whatever you were doing, regardless of how you felt about it. As our older children began to get jobs outside of our home, we saw them live out that important lesson and we were glad that we took the time to insist on teaching it to them at home.

Our goal with the children's academics became mastery. Steve had gotten through school doing the minimum and he regretted not taking the time to truly master his subjects. My school experience much more closely mimicked the home schooling model. My time, studying independently, had allowed me to delve deeply into subjects. Instead of seeing their daily lessons as a "check in the block," we encouraged our children to take the time to redo anything they didn't understand and to take the time necessary to really understand the subject matter.

Just a moment of transparency: My kids stink at math! There, I said it! One of the realities of home schooling is this: Often home schooled children excel in the areas that their parents excel and struggle in the same areas that their parents struggle. Of course, there are exceptions to this rule, but generally speaking, we've have seen this to be true in our family and also, in the many other home schooling families with whom we are associated. It's no surprise that my children excel in writing, speech, and history, while they cringe at math and science lessons.

While all the children were still at home, there were definitely times that I wondered whether we were doing enough. What if they got to college and couldn't keep up with the work? What if they couldn't even get accepted to college? What if they couldn't adapt to learning in a classroom situation? In 2004, Katie graduated from our home school and headed off to college. In some sense, I felt like our reputation as her teachers was on the line and I held my breath in anticipation. What a relief! She did very well, making the Dean's List for both semesters of her freshman year. She did so well, in fact, that she was named to the Who's Who in American College Students. Her experience has proven to be true for the others as well. We'd prayed and worked diligently, hoping that home schooling would prepare our children emotionally, spiritually, and academically, now we had the answer... Home Schooling Worked!

In the beginning of our home schooling adventure, I would have told you that I was super excited about what the children would be learning. Now, looking back over the last nineteen years of home schooling, I've realized that home schooling is as much about what God wants to teach me, as about what I want to teach the children. Steve has always been very good at keeping who he is separate from our children and their home schooling.

That has never been as easy for me. Too often, I found myself feeling like a failure if their academic performance was substandard. I would take it personally if they made a decision that lacked character. I would inwardly fuss and fret over selfish or self-centered attitudes. Steve spent many hours reminding me that the children's bad choices belonged to them; not me. I wish I could say the battle is won, but I'm afraid it will always be an ongoing struggle for me to separate myself and my actions; from those of my children.

The World's Our Classroom!

Sometimes, my over-concern with slip-ups has been almost comical. When Katie and Peter were twelve and eleven, Steve and I had the opportunity to take them to Israel on a trip with his seminary. We thought the trip would be a great educational opportunity for them and a special bonding time for the four of us. Of course, as soon as we arrived at the airport, eleven-year-old Peter hooked up with the bachelors and he spent the three week trip as, "One of the guys." So much for bonding with the parents!

We took off and flew the fourteen hours to Israel. Once we landed, it took several hours to gather our bags, check through customs, and eventually, make our way to the tour buses. After all this time, we still had a several hour bus ride until we finally arrived at our destination for the night. We were exhausted as we headed into the hotel cafeteria for dinner. When Katie and Peter completed their way through the cafeteria line and sat down at the table, Steve looked at their plates in disbelief. On their plates, they each had a whole fish; head, eyes, tail, everything. Steve looked at his children and said, "What's that?" to which they both answered, "Chicken." Steve looked at me and stated, "Home schooling isn't working!"

Now, of course Steve meant that as a joke, but to me ... what a blow! For hours, I laid in bed saying over and over to myself, "Home schooling isn't working ... home schooling isn't working ..." Finally, I woke Steve up from a sound sleep and said, "I think home schooling **is** working, they were just tired!" He didn't even remember what I was talking about, but I was so intertwined in their success or failure, that I had allowed a simple joke to unravel me altogether. Today, I can laugh about my angst, but then, it wasn't so funny.

Nurturing Deeper Family Connections

God has used home schooling to help me to really know my children. I have some children that, like me, can't concentrate in a messy room. Home schooling these children forced me to develop good chore and cleaning routines so that they could do their schoolwork in a peaceful, organized area. I have some children that need more encouragement than their other siblings. Home schooling them required me to be always on the lookout for ways to encourage their work and to remember that those same children take words of discouragement to heart so much more deeply than the others.

I couple of my children are just busy kids—what Steve calls "hyper-diapers." In order for them to do their best work, I had to find ways to help them to burn off energy. Peter, especially, would get so jittery while sitting at the school table that I was forced to come up with a workable solution. After talking with Steve about the problem, we decided that he just needed to balance physical exercise with mental exercise. Every time that Peter finished a subject, I would send him outside to run ten laps around our very large garden. Fall, winter, and spring, he ran those laps. At one point, our neighbor, a dear elderly man that treated my kids like grandchildren, came over to see if Peter was getting in trouble all the time. When we told him what we were doing, he, knowing Peter, agreed that it was a great idea!

Some of my children absolutely thrive on quality time and home schooling certainly provided plenty of that! Those are the children that love to discuss everything that they are learning; they want to share every new discovery with me. My quality time children were the ones that struggled to complete their school assignments if there was any emotional turmoil in our home. Steve and I had to train ourselves to stop what we were doing and address any issues quickly, in order for those children to go on peacefully with their day. I've always wondered about children who have to leave for school with unresolved conflict waiting for them at home. My guess would be that their schoolwork suffers as a consequence.

For my children that craved physical affection, time spent snuggled together each day as they did their read-aloud assignments, filled that need. I've never been a naturally huggy-snuggly person, but I've really grown to love that special time with each child on the couch. Steve loves physical touch, so having our children home all day to hug, tickle, and wrestle on the floor with, was a huge benefit of home schooling.

Because we emphasized character so much as a part of our home schooling, we never really struggled with lousy attitudes. Of course, some days went better than others, but I never had to battle the children to get their work done. They knew what their father and I expected of them and for the most part, they were eager to please us. Without exception, every first day of school was wonderful. Then, Steve and I would have to remind each other that Day #1 was the honeymoon period and it wouldn't always be that easy! Usually, if we had a bad day, I could easily retrace our actions and find the source of the problem. For instance, in 2004 and 2007, when the Red Sox made it to the World Series, we had terrible school days. It was simply because the children had been up too late the nights before. How could I send them to bed when Mike Lowell might hit a winning home run or Jonathon Papelbon might close out the final game with a strike out? Even if it meant rough school days, we had to keep our priorities in order!

More Attentive to Unique Needs

While most of the children excelled at school, we did have one child that really struggled to learn. Our second son, Nate, just couldn't learn to read. It wasn't that he didn't try; he was one of my hardest workers. Reading just didn't make sense to him and every day it was as though he'd never seen the letters or words before. My mom had been a reading specialist and I tried, without success, all of the tips and techniques she shared with me. We read books that encouraged waiting to teach reading to boys until they were older. Steve encouraged me to, "Wait till eight, with Nate." So, we waited until eight, then nine, and then ten ... still nothing changed and Nate's image of himself began to suffer. Children at that age are cruel and even though Nate was at home for school, while he was at church and social events other children began to notice his struggle and humiliate him for not knowing how to read.

Steve and I were committed to doing whatever it took to help Nate learn to read. We were convinced that good reading skills were the foundation of everything else that he would need to learn in order to survive as an adult. Thus began our seventy-five-minute one-way trips to Portland, Maine, four days a week, to take Nate to a reading specialist. His struggle to learn to read, soon, became a great opportunity to teach our children important life lessons.

With me gone for five hours a day taking Nate to the reading tutor, our other children had to pick up the additional load that they were used to me carrying at home. The older girls had extra cooking responsibilities, everyone shared in caring for the younger children, and fun opportunities had to be put on hold. At first, some of the children were envious of the extra time that Nate was getting with Steve or me as we drove him to Portland. We began to sense some grumbling going on behind our backs, and we realized that we were being presented with an important teaching moment.

We called a family conference to discuss what was going on in the family. First, we allowed all of the children to share what they were thinking and feeling. Next, we communicated to the children how we believed God wanted us to view the inconvenient trial that we were experiencing. We reminded the children that God chose us to be a family, the Scheibners, and now, one member of the Scheibner team was suffering. It was as though we were all one body and one of our legs was broken. The rest of the body needed to come alongside that broken leg to help it to heal and be whole. None of the children had thought of it that way. Once they realized how "broken" Nate felt, because of his difficulties in learning, their whole perspective changed. Suddenly, it wasn't about what they were missing, but instead, what they could do to help Nate. Instead of begrudging him the extra time with me, they began to pack him snacks and write him little notes of encouragement. For Nate's part, whenever he achieved milestones, he would earn tokens to spend in the reading school store. He began to use those tokens to purchase little gifts for his brothers and sisters.

For Steve and I, our immediate response to the other children had been to feel bad and to want to placate them. Thankfully, God reminded us of the important life-lesson that needed to be taught. Learning compassion for their brother was a huge lesson for our children. They learned to think of him as more important than themselves and Nate learned to express thankfulness and gratitude, a win-win situation for our whole family.

After seven months with the reading specialist, Nate was reading right on grade level. He has gone on to become one of our most prolific readers and we have to monitor his nighttime reading to make sure he gets enough rest. Every time I catch him with his light on, engrossed in another book, my heart sings! He has developed an immense love for history and loves sharing what he reads with his younger brothers.

In two weeks, Nate will turn eighteen and on the same day he will graduate from high school—a semester early. He has a great part-time job and is looking forward to starting college in the fall. I have no doubt that Nate would have fallen through the cracks of any other educational system. He is a quiet and compliant young man and he would have quietly failed. For him, home schooling made the difference between failure and success!

Creative Curricula

Around the same time that Steve and I were encouraging the children to look beyond their own needs in order to bless and under gird their brother, Nate, we began to use a tool to help our whole family learn to care for each other. We instituted the Loving Your Family Guidelines. These guidelines assigned a different way to show love on each day of the week.

For example, Monday was "Give Day." On that day, we showed love by giving something tangible to someone else. Tuesday was Serve day, another way to show love to others. Wednesday was "Edify Day." Those twenty-four hours were especially important to teach all of us to speak words that built one another up, rather than tearing one another down. Thursday was "Prefer day," probably the hardest day of the week. To prefer someone was to give them something that you had a legitimate right to claim as your own. In our family, the right to the front seat of the car was an especially coveted position and "Prefer Day," provided a great opportunity to show love to someone else. Finally, Friday was Ministry day, a day that we all joined together to minister to another person, or family.

This little tool produced great results in our family. Every Sunday, we would draw names from a hat and whoever you drew-that was the person that you showed love to that week. On Saturday, we would try to guess who had each person, based on the evidence of their giving, serving, edifying, and preferring, throughout the week. I could always tell when one of the little boys had pulled my name. On Monday, I would find a new Army guy on my pillow, (their most treasured possession) and the boys wrote me the sappiest notes on Wednesday.

Our whole family was working together to learn how to show love to one another and to others outside our home. This concentrated time of learning was so helpful when we later had four extra people living in the house and we were all trying to coexist peacefully with one another. Our kids certainly continued to have times of disagreement, but they were learning tangible tools to help them to overcome their own self-centeredness and to instead, love others concretely.

Steve and I never set out to be home school speakers. In fact, our first foray into the home school conference arena was as the entertainment at a major home school event, where we sang The Twelve Days of Home School. We were just busy teaching our own children and trying to be faithfully obedient to God. However, soon other home schooling families began to notice how our children responded to us and how happy we all were with home schooling. Friends called to ask what we were doing to make home schooling fun. For their families, home schooling was unfortunately becoming a chore, not a joy. They sometimes asked if they could just come and watch our family for a day.

Steve and I were never comfortable with the idea of people just copying what our family was doing. We knew that many of the things we did and the choices that we made worked so well because they were God's intent for *our* family. We were never of the mind-set that every family should home school, but we did believe that if a family chose to home school, God wanted them to do it in a way that worked for *their* family and brought glory to Him. We began to pray about ways to help other families without encouraging them just to emulate our home schooling plan.

Soon, we were speaking in various venues, encouraging families to "Home School to an Audience of One." For us, that was what home schooling was really about-pleasing God through our family choices and interactions. We would share the three strands of our family home schooling: Character-building, Service to Others, and Challenging Academics. We shared lots of ideas and strategies. However, we cautioned every audience of the need to pray and discern what was right for their own particular family situation. Families walked away from those times telling us that they were encouraged, and so we continued to travel and speak. Developing teaching for other folks really helped us to stay on track and be careful to be faithful in our own home schooling. Preparing to teach became a built in accountability, for us.

When Steve began the church in Maine, word spread quickly that we were a home schooling family. Soon, other home schooling families joined the ministry at Cornerstone. They felt safe in an environment that encouraged their home schooling and family choices. For many, I think they were surprised by Steve's emphasis on service to others, rather than a family-focus, but they embraced the teaching and their families thrived. Because of that service-oriented, others-oriented teaching, Cornerstone never became a "home school exclusive" type of church, but instead was a good mix of all educational philosophies.

We're winding up our home schooling years. When Nate graduates in two weeks, we will only have three children left at home. Lately, we find ourselves wondering what it will be like during the three years that we are only home schooling Taylor. We tease the older children that we will get season tickets to Fenway Park and home school Tate between innings of the Red Sox games. However that time turns out, we wouldn't trade our years of home schooling for anything. The opportunity, and sometimes challenge, of being with our children twenty-four hours a day, has provided character lessons for us and valuable teaching materials to share with others. We definitely won't regret not spending enough time with our children.

For us, home schooling works!

Chapter 11

Family First

Steve's story is really our family's story. Who he is as a man and a leader, in large part, was developed as he led and nurtured our family. God has used Steve's roles as a husband and father to develop and strengthen his convictions and to provide the working models of what we would later turn into the Characterhealth teaching curricula. Each child, in their own special way, has had a part in building our family testimony and credibility.

I wish I had a dime for all of the times that Steve and I have been asked about the size of our family. To us, eight children doesn't seem like a very big deal, but to "normal" people, the size of our family is an anomaly. True, there are much larger families in the public eye, but I think most people see them as an exception, perhaps as celebrities. Folks see us as a normal family, just swollen to a disproportionate size!

We Started Out Small

When we were first married, Steve and I didn't set out to have a large family. In fact, in our pre-marriage "Oh-I-can't-wait-until-we're-parents" discussions, we generally focused on having two, or maybe three, children at the most. We both grew up in families where we were the youngest of three children and our siblings were quite a bit older. I was the only girl and Steve was the only boy. Neither of us had been encouraged to develop any type of close family relationships with our siblings, we just all co-existed at one address. We knew for sure that we wanted a closer family dynamic than the ones that we had grown up with, but we didn't necessarily think that we needed lots of children to reach that goal.

In fact, there were times that one, or sometimes both of us, felt that having children was a terrible idea. When we were first married, we lived in a small community filled with other young Navy couples. To me, it seemed as if everyone else had a baby, except me ... and those babies were *sooooo* cute! I loved their little useless feet and their adorable clothes and how they cuddled with me, and, and, and ... I probably mentioned having a baby about fifty times a day. After a couple weeks of these gentle comments (Steve saw it as nagging, go figure), he forbade me to mention the word *baby* in our home. He reminded me that we had decided to wait until flight training was completed before we started our family and the constant baby requests were making him crazy. All of our friends were pushing us to have a baby, as well, and he was definitely feeling as if everyone was ganging up on him. Actually, as soon as I stopped talking about babies all of the time, I really began to enjoy the freedom that Steve and I had, and which our "parenting friends" lacked.

When we arrived at our next duty station, I began working in a daycare. Out of the blue, Steve began talking about having a baby and this time, I couldn't think of a less appealing idea. I worked with whiny, disobedient children all day and I didn't want to come home to my own at night. Again, we weren't on the same page about children and when Steve began to come visit me at work, he really started to understand my point of view. If it wasn't for our relationship with Wayne and Debbie Smith and time spent with their cheerful, obedient children, we might have stayed childless forever.

Nevertheless, the extended Scheibner family began in April of 1987, and we never looked back. We certainly didn't realize, when Katie was born, that we would eventually have eight children, but parenting just seemed to come naturally to both of us. I think that Steve and I were somewhat surprised by how easily we transitioned from a family of three, to a family of four, to a family of five, etc. The changes in our family just seemed like a normal progression. We were excited with the addition of each new baby.

"God Habits" Build Happy Kids

Over the years, Steve and I have spent a great deal of time talking about parenting and the parenting process. As we developed the Parenting Matters course and as Steve wrote his doctoral dissertation, we wanted to be careful to accurately portray biblical parenting, as well as the choices we made in our home that helped to develop a character-healthy family. I think that sometimes people have looked at our family, and the family dynamic they observe, and they have tried to excuse away the results. It would be easier to believe that our children were just really mellow and calm and that's why they seemed so obedient. Or perhaps, we were so militaristic and controlling that our children obeyed us out of fear. Neither of these rationalizations are a good explanation of what makes our family tick. The truth is this: Steve and I both take parenting, family relationships, and the importance of glorifying God very seriously. Because of this, everything we do in those three realms comes under intense scrutiny. We try to help one another parent with the end result of glorifying God in the forefront of our minds.

Even writing those last couple of sentences, I think, *Wow, we sound so serious.* But honestly, it isn't that we spend all day worrying that we might be doing something wrong, it is more of a habit of life at this point. For so long, we've asked our children, and ourselves "What's the value at stake here?" that living out that question is now just second nature to us. We're certainly not perfect as parents and there are days that I wish that I could just push a reset button. However, both Steve and I have found that as we try to walk in faithful obedience to the Lord, our children are more likely to want to walk in that faithful obedience, as well.

Life in a large family is an interesting phenomenon. In some ways, we're like a small community all living under one roof. Actually, sometimes we're like a small science experiment. If one child gets it—whatever *it* may be—they all catch it. All eight of our children are vastly different from each other. All eight of our children are strongly opinionated and exceedingly verbal! (I think they got that from their father!) Each boy and girl in our home thinks that his or her way is the way to go. Throw into the mix their father and I, and you could have a total anarchy. Very early on, we decided that our home would not operate that way. Both Steve and I hated the movies and TV shows that portrayed large families as one mess after another, with an overwhelmed mother and a clueless dad. We knew for certain, that if God had given us these children, and He had, He wanted us to raise them in a way that pointed to Him.

Living in the small community of our family and parenting our children has provided many of the foundational lessons of our parenting curriculum. One of the most important modules that we teach in the "Nine Practices of the Pro-Active Parent," is a module that concerns personality and the role that different personalities play in the decision making process. Steve and I believe, and we have taught our children, that although we have one set standard for character and behavior in our home, each of us may arrive at that standard via a different route. Areas of specific strengths and weaknesses, as well as the lenses through which we view life, in essence, our personalities, are what will determine these different routes.

The three lenses, or personalities, that assist us in the decision-making process are the *thinker,* the *doer,* and the *feeler.* These three, vastly different, types of people make up our world, and for the Scheibners, these vastly different personalities make up our home. A well-balanced person would really be a nice blend of all three of these personality types, but we have found, through our teaching and especially through the experimental nature of our home, that most people lean strongly in one direction or another.

Thinkers Have Already "Thunked" It!

A thinker is the type of person who has all of their dominoes in order, all their ducks in a row. These types of folks are generally speaking highly organized and methodical in how they approach life. I am a thinker. Thinkers don't do well with spontaneity, sudden changes, or the curve balls of life. I don't do well with spontaneity, sudden changes, or curve balls. Thinkers love to think and rethink a plan to develop what seems, to them, to be the best course of action and then they are doggedly stubborn in sticking with that plan. When a thinker, and I'm no exception to this rule, gets interrupted in their thought process, they have to go all the way back to the beginning and start over. Thinkers love routine, order, and structure. Thinker children become very attached to the, "But we've always done it that way," things of life.

When Steve and I were first married, my thinker tendencies drove him crazy. Sometimes, when he asked me a question and received no forthcoming response, he thought I was a little slow. He just couldn't understand what was going on in my brain. However, when we had children and he began to recognize the same tendencies in their actions, the light bulb came on for him. He realized that the children and I weren't just slow, or stalling, we were processing. For our thinker children, we soon noticed that they tended toward delayed obedience. They spent so much time considering all of the ramifications of their obedience that they were slow to actually get to it. Truthfully, sometimes that's how I am in my walk with the Lord. I spend so much time considering all the steps necessary to enact change in my life that I never seem to get around to actually changing.

My daughter, Emma, is so much like me. She is a total thinker, which serves her quite well in her career as a chef. Outside of work though, her extreme thinker tendencies aren't always such a plus. To add to the mix, Emma married a thinker husband. Sometimes when we ask them a question, both Steve and I are awed by their total thinker paralysis. Their heads tip off to the side, their mouths fall open, and if they were a pinball machine, they would have *TILT* written on their foreheads. It is comical to see them both lock up and try to organize all of the various dominoes that we have knocked over in their minds. I sometimes wonder what will happen if they end up with a whole house full of doer, or even feeler, children!

Much like their sister Emma, my sons Nate and Tate (Taylor) are thinker boys. Steve and I have had to learn, over the years, to give them lead-time, or what we call pre-activity time, to make decisions or get motivated to take action. I find myself telling both of them, "You don't have to think about this, just get moving and do it!" We know that as the future goal-setters in their own homes, both boys will need to be decisive and timely leaders, so we are committed to teaching them not to use their thinker tendencies as an excuse for delayed decision-making. Instead, they need to learn to harness those great organizational skills in order to reach their full potential.

Doers Don't Always Get It Done

Doers are the opposite extreme of the personality spectrum from thinkers. Doers are those people who come up with a hundred ideas a day. They are great starters, although not such great finishers. Steve always says that doer husbands are the ones with half-finished projects all over their homes. Steve is a total doer and he didn't put the final piece of molding up in my Pennsylvania kitchen until the week we were moving out. For a doer, the joy of life is found in the launching of a new idea. It took me years to realize that 99 percent of Steve's ideas were just in his head. He didn't really intend for them to ever happen. At one time or another, Steve has mentioned selling everything and living on a boat to save money, building a home with no electricity or running water, becoming a missionary pilot, and the list goes on and on. As a thinker, every time he mentioned a new idea, I tried to find a way to make it work. Remember, thinkers have to plan ahead. As you can imagine, our two personalities clashed often until we realized just how differently we approached life.

Raising doer children can be especially challenging. Peter and Stephen, Jr. are our two total doers. It isn't that their ideas aren't good; it's just that there are so many of them. Stephen, especially, always seems to have something new to attempt that is the latest and greatest thing going. When the rest of the family doesn't embrace his new idea with the same enthusiasm, he is plunged into the depths of despair. I think that I've mellowed with age. Stephen's doer ideas usually just seem funny to me. When he shows up at 9:00 p.m. with a cookie recipe in hand, prepared to go begin a new project, I recognize that it's just that he's had an idea and what time it is doesn't really matter to him. When Peter was younger, though, some of his ideas made me daydream about enrolling him in military school.

Once, when I had arranged a babysitter for the day, Peter's doer tendencies came out in full force. He told the babysitter that he was allowed to play alone downstairs (True) and that all of his building toys were downstairs. (Again, true) He assured her that he would keep himself busy with an appropriate activity and that she could just relax and enjoy a movie, upstairs, with the other children. (Not so true) Who wouldn't believe a charming boy like Peter?

Peter's "appropriate" activity was only appropriate in his mind. You see, he had been thinking about one of his great ideas all morning. He remembered how much fun the water slide we had visited the previous summer had been and he was determined to recreate that great time at home. He was sure that the other children would thank him for their own water slide. Unfortunately, it was February in Pennsylvania, so he recreated the waterslide inside, in our carpeted basement. He took our toddler slide and propped it up on some toy bricks. Then he gathered all the necessary supplies. Next, he called his younger sister downstairs to join him. Emma was always Peter's first choice to join him in his criminal activity. When the babysitter came down to check on the children, she found my daughter, fully clothed and sliding down the toddler slide, while Peter poured pitcher after pitcher of water to make it a water slide. The carpet and Emma were soaked and the mess overwhelmed the babysitter. Peter just couldn't understand what all the fuss was about. Another doer idea gone down the drain! (*Pun intended!*)

Burnt Offerings vs. Timely Obedience

No surprises here, Steve and I found that our doer children tended to give us what we called "burnt offerings," instead of timely obedience. Because they always had, what seemed to them, to be a better idea, they tried to replace obedience with that better idea. For example, sometimes I would send Stephen to bed, only to have him reappear to tell me that he had just reorganized the DVD shelf. In reality, as he passed the shelf he had an idea like: "Those DVDs would be easier to find if they were alphabetized," or "I should put all the Disney films together." Then, because the idea became the primary focus in his mind, bedtime was relegated to the back shelf and now here he was, presenting me with an accomplished task, but not the one I had sent him to accomplish. Both he and Peter were always surprised when I didn't thank them for their burnt offerings. They were even more surprised, and often offended, when they found themselves in trouble for disobedience.

With my thinker children, I spent time motivating them to get moving. Doer children have no trouble getting moving! Instead, for our doer children, my tagline became, "You don't have to like, agree with, or even embrace what I'm telling you to do. Don't change or improve the idea. Just Do It!" Slowly but surely, both of our boys are learning to put their ideas into the proper priority and to be characterized by obedience and responsibility.

It's an interesting dynamic, but I'm probably more merciful toward our doer children and Steve tends to show more mercy toward the thinkers. Perhaps, it's our years of learning to function with one another and our extreme thinker/doer tendencies that has given us compassion for the opposite personality children.

The Feeler's Emotional Climate

Feelers are the third category of personalities we teach about in our parenting course. Our family really has only one true feeler. Sweet Baleigh is the emotional barometer for our home. Feelers are the people who are in tune with the emotional climate of a situation. They are aware of when someone is feeling excluded or ostracized. Without feelers, it would be a boring/methodical thinker world or a "roll-em-over-and-keep-going" doer world.

Sometimes, I feel sorry for Baleigh as she navigates her way in a predominantly thinker/doer family. *Sometimes.* There are other times that the strong feeler emotions she embraces make me, as a thinker, want to pull my hair out. All teenage girls are emotional to one degree or another, but Steve and I are convinced that feeler teenage girls get more than their share of the emotional DNA.

Besides being aware of the emotional climate surrounding them, feelers are also prone to take second party offense for others. Baleigh is no exception to this rule. Sometimes she stirs up trouble where none exists, simply because she assumes that because she would be offended by a particular situation, therefore her siblings must be offended, or hurt, as well. Steve and I have worked hard to teach Baleigh how to practice self-control with her emotions and that hard work is paying off. Sometimes now, we can watch her swallow hard, fold her hands, and squelch the inappropriate emotions that she is feeling at the moment.

If you add up the children that I've mentioned, you may notice that we're missing two children. It's interesting, but our oldest daughter, Katie, has always been hard to categorize into a personality type. Because she was the oldest child and a female child as well, she would seem to be a doer. She has always been a take-charge, "we-should-do-it- my-way" child, somewhat the second-mommy syndrome. On the other hand, as the oldest child and a female, she was always very aware of fairness and any inequity in the home, more of a feeler tendency. As well, she was a list maker and inventory keeper, which reminded us of me, the thinker. We've never spent much time or given much credence to birth order, but in Katie's case, we saw that her position as the oldest definitely influenced her personality or the lens through which she viewed life.

How about Molly? Molly was really our most evenly balanced child. She's a really nice mix of all three personality types. She works hard to have all of her life-dominoes in place, but Molly also loves spontaneity and surprises. She is somewhat of a daredevil and risk-taker. She can sometimes be our biggest dreamer, but usually she comes up with a concrete plan to fulfill those dreams. When she was sixteen, she decided to spend part of her summer in South Africa. We weren't sure how that would work, but we gave her our blessing to pursue her dream. Within twenty-four hours, she found a tutoring job that provided the money she would need. She researched and obtained all the necessary shots. She compared the pros and cons of purchasing a ticket or flying stand-by, and finally, she flew stand-by, all by herself, to Capetown, South Africa. What a wonderful merging of the thinker and doer lenses of life. To Molly's friends, she became the go-to person when they had a problem, or needed a listening ear. She never felt adequate for that responsibility, but her humility in that area has allowed her to be used by God as a minister to her friends.

Growing in God Together

Having our children as an ever-ready test bed of parenting training has been an invaluable tool. Although nothing we believed prior to having our first child has radically changed, God has used the children and their various personalities to grow both Steve and I and to help us to fine-tune what we teach to other parents. Neither of us had a basis of Christian family life on which to base our beliefs; God's Word was sufficient to teach us all that we needed to know. God's Word continues to teach us daily more about how to parent our own children and encourage other parents as they train their families.

We love all of our children dearly, but it was obvious to us, from the first moment that we held Baby Katie in our arms, that it would be very easy for us to become child-centered. We knew, from our study of Scripture, that God had designed families to be parent centered. Our children were intended to be welcome members of the family team, but they were never meant to be the center of attention. We believed that as our children grew in their respect for us, as their parents, they would grow in responsibility and respect for God, as their authority, also.

Boy, is it ever hard to stay parent centered! As a mom, every part of my existence seemed to be about providing the best possible environment, teaching, and care, for my children. Keeping Steve as a priority was a difficult task. However, Steve and I both saw clearly that when we kept our marriage as the priority relationship in the home, our children were much more secure, trusting, and ultimately, happy. Sometimes as Steve and I headed out the door to spend some much needed mommy/daddy time, the children would chorus that it "just wasn't fair" that we would go off and leave them. We still left!

Ahh ... fairness. This is a huge trap for all families and the Scheibner family is no exception. If there was one lesson that I tried to hammer home, it was the lesson that we weren't as concerned about fairness, as we were concerned with consistency. With eight children, if I had tried to make sure that everything was absolutely Even-Steven, we would never have gotten anything accomplished. Also, we would have been broke. I wish that I could tell you that my children have embraced that teaching wholeheartedly, but we find ourselves still teaching and re-teaching that lesson, even today.

Our oldest children were somewhat all of a certain type. They were all gifted musicians; we had piano players, a flutist, a violinist, a would-be cello player, and guitar players. They loved acting and participated in many productions. They were involved in teen political rallies and campaigned for their chosen politicians. However, they were NOT athletic. We tried various sports through the local YMCA, but they were just NOT athletes.

Then came our youngest three children. Our daughter Baleigh is an extremely talented swimmer and is in demand by coaches from other sports because of her athletic ability and reputation as a coachable athlete. Stephen and Taylor are both outstanding baseball players and Stephen has consistently played for the All-Star team. This is his first year on the swim team and he is just as competitive there. Taylor, at age ten, is an up and coming boxer. That's just how God made those children.

Enter the "fairness trap." Suddenly, our oldest children were bemoaning the fact that they never got to be on any sports teams. Forget the hours spent driving them to music lessons and play practices; their life was incomplete because they never received a Varsity letter. Oh my word!

Don't let yourself be sucked into the fairness trap. Our children absolutely must learn to be happy for the good things that come into their sibling's lives. Children, who never learn that important character lesson, will become adults who are jealous of the blessings that others receive. Steve and I saw that unfortunate dynamic played out, over and over, in our ministry at the church.

It's funny to us just how overwhelming a large family seems to most people. So many folks have said something to Steve and I along the lines of "I could never do it... I'm just not patient enough." That one always makes us laugh. Steve would never claim to be the most patient man on earth and I'm not even patient enough to wait to distribute Christmas gifts. As soon as I buy them, I find a chance to give them out, then I have to buy more, which I give out, etc., etc. No, God didn't give us so many children because He knew that we were such patient parents, He gave us children to act as sandpaper to wear off the rough edges of our impatience.

Before we had children, Steve and I were sticklers for being on time. One of the Navy lessons he learned that he then transferred to our home was this: If you're on time, you're five minutes late. We really tried to be faithful to that creed because we both realized that punctuality was an important, although often overlooked, character quality. Enter eight children. For us, these types of situations offered opportunities that proved whether or not we really believed what we said; or were our actions only based on the expedience of the moment?

Getting ten people out the door and into the van in order to arrive at church, doctor's appointments, or music lessons, was no small feat. If we weren't prepared for success, too often, we failed and our failure showed up in late entrances, made more obvious by the large number in our group. I adopted a saying and used it to remind myself to be organized. "When you're late and rushing; you're harsh and hasty." I realized that running behind often caused me to run at the mouth, as well. Too often, I found myself harshly addressing the children and saying things that were hurtful and degrading, simply because my lack of preparation had caused us to be running behind.

When all of the children were still at home, the Scheibner family represented a major troop movement. We spent time teaching the oldest four to take care of their buddy, one of the youngest four. While I was still ultimately responsible to make sure that everyone had what was needed, each of the older four made sure that their buddy was completely clothed and buckled into the car, on time. I had helpers on the team, the older children learned responsibility, and the younger kids loved the special attention from their buddy.

Despite our best efforts, we did have a couple of "left behind" failures. Once, when I was cooking at a kid's camp, Steve came to join me from a campground in another town. He loaded up the fifteen-passenger van with our kids and some extra teenagers. As he was driving to the camp, he had a funny feeling in the pit of his stomach. He called out, "Stephen, let me know that you're here." No answer, so he called again. Finally, one of the teenagers piped up and told him that Stephen Jr. wasn't in the car. Somehow, he had been left behind. Steve and that vanload of kids arrived where I was working and the kids all filed through the kitchen saying, "Dad has something he doesn't want to tell you." Fortunately, about that time, a friend from the other campground called to say that he had found something that belonged to us in the bathroom. Poor little Stephen had run to the bathroom and when he came out the van was gone.

Another time didn't work out exactly as we had planned. Our second daughter, Emma, has always been a social butterfly. Every week after church, we would all be loaded in the big, blue van waiting to go home for lunch and there would be no Emma. Steve and I coached her, reminded her, and encouraged her, all to no avail. We decided to teach her a memorable lesson. The next Sunday, we all loaded in the van and waited for Emma to come out the front door of the church. As soon as she appeared, Steve drove away, leaving her behind. We drove around the block and returned, hoping to find a repentant daughter, distraught that she had been left behind. Instead, we found Emma surrounded by a group of adults, all bartering over who would get to take her home for lunch. Emma was weighing her options, not concerned about us leaving her behind, at all.

Now that three of the kids are married and gone from home, and another one is away at college, when they all come home to visit it is an absolute riot. We gather around the table and they share "True Confessions" of the crimes they committed that they think we don't know about. Remember, Steve and I were already teens when we became Christians; these kids have been Christians since they were children. Their idea of criminal activity is laughable!

The older group sometimes bemoans the horrors of life in a large family. Two major complaints come to mind. The first is this: We had four beautiful little girls. So, I did what any proud mama would do; I dressed them in matching outfits, on occasion. (They would say on too many occasions!) Little did I realize that I was damaging their psyche for life. Poor Molly bore the brunt of the embarrassment. While in South Africa, a total stranger came up to her and said, "I remember you. I visited a church in Pennsylvania and you were in the pew with your sisters. You were all so cute and adorable in your MATCHING DRESSES ..." *Oh, the horror of it all!* Their second complaint surrounds my perceived over-usage of oatmeal.

To listen to the four oldest, you would think that all I ever served those kids was oatmeal. Coincidentally, the married girls often call me for my recipes; maybe they didn't survive on just oats after all. If all our children can find to complain about is cute clothing and a good hot breakfast, I think we did Okay!

Being in a large family certainly has its challenges, but for us, we wouldn't trade it for anything. The family closeness that Steve and I missed as children has been realized in our own family. Working hard to teach our children important, God-honoring character has taught us to consistently elevate virtues over feelings in our own lives. As God trained us, we trained our children, and that training has multiplied and grown into the fruitful ministry of Characterhealth. Back in our newlywed days, when we were discussing the theory of parenting, I could have never imagined how busy and full our lives would be today. Now, I'm anxious for the next phase.

With eight children, three of them already married, the future opportunities for our family's continued growth are absolutely mind-boggling.

Chapter 12

"Watch Me, and Watch God!"

We are often asked to reflect on how our lives have changed since September 11, 2001. As I've shared in this story, so many major changes have occurred that sometimes the little things get lost in the shuffle. Let me share some of those little things with you here. Perhaps of equal importance are the things that didn't change because Steve wasn't on the flight.

If Steve had been on Flight 11 that day, our cord of three strands would have been radically affected. For the church, Cornerstone Baptist would have most likely shut its doors. Being in its infancy, the loss of the Senior Pastor would have been a devastating blow. Instead, this congregation is a thriving and viable ministry to the community here in Maine.

For the Navy, ten-thousand sailors would have never interacted with the Core Values course. Steve saw that course as pre-evangelism and it has opened the door to many spiritual conversations with those who attended. For some, that course and their time with Steve may have been their only interaction with Christian concepts and character.

For our family and parenting, September 25, 2001, became an important date. Two weeks after the terrorist hijackings, a little boy was born in Guatemala City, Guatemala. With two children already placed in foster care, his young mother put him into the state-run adoption/foster care system, as well. Fifteen months later, that little boy became Taylor Christian Scheibner, our eighth child. We hadn't been pursuing adoption, but God knew that he belonged in our family. If Steve had been on Flight 11, the court would never have allowed me, a single mother of seven, to adopt him. *We are blessed.*

Life looks different now around the Scheibner house. On September 11, 2001, my oldest child was fourteen and the youngest child was two. We had two in braces and one in diapers. Today, there's nary a diaper to be found, and although we still have two in braces, at least it's a different two.

On September 11, 2001, we had nine people living at home. In the ten years following that time the number swelled to fourteen with the addition of a single mom, her two children, and a troubled teenager. Now, there are only six of us left at home. Our three oldest children are married and off on their own. Molly, child number four, is a senior in college and Nate will begin college next August. Baleigh is a junior in high school and lives her life to swim, fiddle, and lead worship music.

Soon it will be just Steve, me, and our two youngest boys. We're enjoying this time with the youngest children. Life isn't necessarily any less demanding, but the stress has been replaced by joy and excitement in our family ministry.

Sometimes our children wonder why their dad is in such demand and why both he and I have to travel so often. They realize our family doesn't look like many of the other families they see. I always remind them of this simple truth: *To those whom much has been given; much is required.* God has given our family so much. After all He's done for us, there is nothing that their dad and I wouldn't do for Him. When God chose Katie, Peter, Emma, Molly, Nate, Baleigh, Stephen, and Tate, to be our children, He chose them to join us in enjoying His blessings, as well as joining us in the responsibilities that we bear as ministers of the gospel.

Unleashed to Serve

On September 11, 2001, I was simply a stay-at-home mom and home educator. Now I write, teach, and speak at churches and conferences. I couldn't have imagined then, what my life would look like now.

Steve is just as busy as ever. He still flies for the airlines, drills with the Navy, and now he travels to speak and teach all over the country. He's still an involved dad and together we embarrass our children at their sporting events. People ask him how he does it all and the answer is this: When God is behind what you're doing; God will multiply your hours.

Throughout the years, I have had women tell me that they couldn't stand to be married to Steve with his crazy lifestyle. For me, I couldn't stand to *not* be married to him. God knit us together a long time ago and He has taught me how to be a helper suitable to the man He gave me.

Before September 11, 2001, I often found myself covetous of Steve's time. I always wanted him to be home more, after all, the trend in Christian teaching at the time was the premise that men needed to be home continually. I know of some very spiritual men who quit their jobs to start home businesses. On the two-year anniversary of September 11th, I watched Steve speak at a large church in Texas. As I was sitting in the pew, the still small voice of the Holy Spirit impressed this thought on my heart, "Let him go." I realized then, perhaps for the first time, that Steve didn't belong to me, he belonged first and foremost to God. The man I married was no tame tiger, and I needed to unleash him to fulfill his God-given calling. I knew that God had prepared me to be capable and to manage the home front so that Steve could minister for Him, now was the time to embrace that role wholeheartedly. Freeing Steve to minister wherever and whenever God called has freed our whole family from expectations. Now, when Steve is home he is 100 percent home. When he must leave, he can be 100 percent available elsewhere, knowing that we're at home cheering him on and keeping things running smoothly.

At the time of this writing, Tim Tebow is splashed on the pages of the news each week. He just keeps on winning games, even though the sportscasters and coaches continue saying he has no chance. He is boldly standing for Christ and unapologetic in his testimony. Many don't understand him, but while they are saying, "He can't," Tebow continues to say, "Watch me, and watch God!"

Steve Scheibner spent his life hearing, "You can't." But, like Tim Tebow, he is unapologetic and bold in his stand for Christ. Many don't understand him, but while they are saying, "He can't," Steve, too, continues to say, "Watch me, and watch God!"

In My Seat (the book) is not the end of the story for Steve; it's just more of the story God is writing in his life. I have no doubt that Steve will continue to: "Seek, trust, and glorify God, through humble service and continual prayer. And to raise up qualified disciples as quickly as possible." I know, without a doubt, that someday, Steve Scheibner will hear, "Well-done, my good and faithful servant."

Afterword

Shortly after the film, "In My Seat," was released, I began receiving phone calls, emails, and text messages asking me if a book was forthcoming. At first, I dismissed the notion of writing a book about my experience as self-serving. Besides, who would be interested in reading about a pilot who almost died? Then, the film went "viral," with more than 14,000 YouTube hits each day, week after week, with no signs of slowing down. It was clear, from that moment forward, that this film was different. "In My Seat" is not your usual internet sensation, featuring a boy and a bike ramp, that ends in predictable catastrophe. There are no gross bodily functions being exploited like so many other YouTube offerings, and the film runs a full 15 minutes, which goes well beyond the average American attention span of two to three minutes max. It is apparent that this documentary is striking a cord with people, deep inside. I have received well over a thousand emails from total strangers and they all start with the word, Wow! Grateful viewers are writing with tears in their eyes, while they describe the life changing experience that "In My Seat" has been for them.

At the time of this writing over 1.6 million computers have logged on to "In My Seat." Since YouTube only registers the first hit from a computer, there is no telling exactly how many people have actually viewed the film, but 1.6 million computer hits translates into roughly 5 million people. More than 1500 churches played the film in just the first 10 weeks after it's release, which accounts for another million viewers. The success of this project, to date, is truly phenomenal. My son, Peter, is a filmmaker in college, and "In My Seat" was his undergrad senior project. Not bad for a first effort... his future as a filmmaker looks bright.

The details behind the film are significant as well. The film has been viewed in every country around the world including: Iran, Yemen, and North Korea. I spoke with Peter recently and he informed me that there was a special viewing of the film at the Vatican... how cool is that! Just last week, he received an email from the Vatican telling him how much the priests enjoyed the film. Men prefer the film by a 56% to 44% margin over women, and the film is being viewed mostly by those in the 45 to 65 year old age bracket. Texan's are watching the film more than any other state and the vast majority of viewers stay with the film for the entire fifteen minutes, which is extraordinary. The portion of the film that garners the most attention is the "Life Objective," toward the end. Statistical analysis shows us that viewers are rewinding the film to re-read that spiritual life objective which I wrote more than 20 years ago. My "Life Objective" is the most valuable tool I have (Besides the Word of God,) in my life to help guide daily spiritual, emotional, and physical decisions. In fact, one of the most requested conferences I teach is called "Second Mile Leadership." This course is designed to teach men how to lead in their homes, churches, and workplaces. During a "Second Mile Leadership" event, I show each participant how to write his own spiritual life objective. To date, I have helped more than 10,000 men write their own life objectives.

So, why did Megan, my wife, write the book and not me? For our entire life together (that now spans 28 years and counting,) Megan has been a sort of Ringmaster to the Scheibner Circus. She observes first hand everything that goes on in my life from the ground floor. She is one of the smartest people I know and she is extremely well read. Her mastery of the English language is extensive and she is a gifted writer. She is warm, funny, and transparent. The things I have grown to love about her over the years are the very things I wanted you to experience first hand, through her writing. As you read, and re-read, *In My Seat,* you will see yourself as God sees you, mainly because you will see the Scheibner's as God sees the Scheibner's, thanks to Megan's poignant prose. Her perspective was the right lens through which to view the events leading up to September 11th and beyond. For me to write a book about myself would have been too self-serving, even for a pilot, and believe me, I know a lot of self-serving aviators. Since, you have made it this far, I know you agree that Megan was the right choice to write *In My Seat.*

"In My Seat" (the film) is having a profound impact on those who watch it. The film is more than just a history lesson or documentary about a near death experience. The film is a total immersion into the purpose of life. At the end of the film I say, "I know what it is like to have someone die in my place, not just once, but twice." Although Tom McGuinness died in the pilot seat that I should have occupied on September 11th, 2001, Tom would be the first person to tell you that he did not die to pay for my sins. Tom McGuinness had a solid testimony of faith in Jesus Christ. I am convinced that Tom went straight into the arms of the Lord on 9/11. In fact, Tom's widow, Cheryl, travels around the country speaking to various groups about the power of forgiveness and the power of restoration that only God can provide, through a relationship with Jesus Christ. But Tom did not pay for, nor could he pay for, my sins. The main focus in the film is not Tom, but Jesus. The other Man who died in my place is far more significant, than Tom. Uniquely qualified, Jesus hung, suffered, and bled, on a cross, to pay the price for my sins and the sins of all mankind. He rose from the grave on the third day and reconciled God, the Father, to mankind, for all who will accept the free gift of His Son. As I travel around the country accompanying the film, I have witnessed scores of people responding to the Gospel by committing their lives to Christ. God is using this film in a powerful way.

After the film is shown, I share what the late Paul Harvey used to call "the rest of the story." I take my audiences to John chapter 21 and I share a very simple message about how quickly life can change. People have asked me over the years how my life has changed since the events of September 11th. I usually respond by telling them that God has developed a very deep sense of urgency in my life. I want to get the most out of my days... not the most for me, rather the most for God. John 21 sets a scene, shortly after the resurrection of Jesus, where seven of the twelve disciples are together and Peter decides to go fishing. On a whim, Peter announces his desire to go catch some fish; the other six decide to tag along. Very quickly, we learn that although they fished all night, they caught nothing. By verse 4, of John 21, Jesus arrives on the beach to confront His disciples with a profound truth. They must start living more like "Borrowed Time Believers" and less like "Someday Saints." When Jesus first called these men, He singled them out to become fishers of men, not fishers of fish. In chapter 21, in the shadow of the greatest life-changing event of all history, we find seven of the most important men on the planet in their little boat fishing. It is no surprise that they caught nothing that night. Their "Someday" attitude of life was not pleasing to the Lord and He intended to do something about it. In the next 12 verses, He will remind these seven repeatedly that they are living on borrowed time. They must live each day with a renewed sense of urgency. No longer should they be fishing for the stuff of life that so quickly rots and stinks, like fish; rather, they should be transforming the world, one life at a time, with eternity in mind. At this point, I ask my audiences three questions, the same three questions that Jesus asked His disciples in John 21, and the same three questions God was confronting me with on September 11th, 2001. . First: "What are you doing here?" When Jesus shows up on the beach, at first He doesn't utter a word. His mere presence at daybreak implies the question to those in the boat "What are you doing here?" How would you answer that question? What purpose does your life serve? What difference are you making on this planet? How does your life bring glory to God? The answer to these questions is important. Every life is precious and God has a plan for every life to bring glory to Him, even yours! If you keep His plan for your life at arms length, then you are living like a Someday Saint. However, if you are eager to serve God and follow His plan for your life, no matter where it might take you, then you are living like a Borrowed Time Believer.

The second question I ask my audience is: "What are you fishing for in life?" Just like the disciples, it is easy for us to become distracted and begin to fish for the wrong stuff in life. There is nothing wrong with fishing for fish, unless you have been uniquely qualified to fish for men. In verse 5, Jesus asked them if they have caught any fish… a curious question considering who asked it. Jesus already knew the answer before He asked the question, so the question must be for the benefit of the disciples. In other words, "What are you fishing for?" How would you answer that question? What is the main objective of your life? Are you fishing for comfort, acceptance, security, love, or any of a million other temporal pursuits? Or, are you fishing to please God, in the spirit of 2 Corinthians 5:9, that reminds us to make it our ambition, whether home or away, to be pleasing to God. I have to confess, on September 11th, 2001, I was fishing for a lot of stuff that did not have eternal significance.

The final question I ask those in attendance is: "What do you love more than Jesus?" Verses 15-17, of John 21, lay out a very clear mandate for followers of Christ to set their priorities right. Jesus confronted Peter three times with the same question, "Do you love me more than these?" I believe Jesus was asking Peter about the fish he just caught. In a very straightforward manner, Jesus looked directly into Peter's eyes and asked him if he loved God more than the 153 fish that Jesus helped Peter catch in verse 6. Peter responded as we would expect him to respond with, "Yes Lord, you know that I love you." Again in verse 16, Jesus repeated the question, and again Peter responded in the affirmative, but something was not right in this exchange. The men were talking at cross-purposes and verse 17 will reveal the discrepancy. All along, Jesus had been using one Greek word for love and Peter has been responding with a completely different Greek word. Jesus used the word Agape, which is a divine type of love. Agape is an unconditional love that implies there are no strings attached. Peter on the other hand, used the word Phileo, which is where we get the name for the City of Philadelphia, otherwise known as the City of Brotherly Love. Phileo is a conditional type of love. Jesus was asking Peter for a deeper love than Peter was willing to give. Jesus wanted Peter to move from being a Someday Saint to embracing the role of a Borrowed Time Believer. As I share the "rest of the story," lives, including my own, are being changed. We sometimes call the film "The Little Film That Could." God has taken a simple, fifteen-minute student project, and transformed it into a world-wide tool for His kingdom. The film is forcing those who watch it to ask themselves, "What am I doing here?" "What am I fishing for?" and, "What do I love more than Jesus?" How you and I respond to those questions will determine if we are a Someday Saint or a Borrowed Time Believer.

Finally, I have crossed paths with a number of men and women in the last year that are talking about God's purpose for their lives. Unlike similar conversations I have had throughout my lifetime, these conversations are different. I believe God is raising up men and women who want to see the world changed for the cause of Christ. These men and women are big picture thinkers and doers, who are eager to sacrifice their time and personal fortunes to see the world transformed through Jesus. I count Megan and I among those who want to see our world changed for Christ, and we are willing to give up everything we have to see it happen in our lifetime. I truly believe that I will see a substantial transformation in the lives of parents, regarding their children, in my lifetime. Megan and I started Characterhealth Corporation to equip parents to train a new generation of courageous, Christlike, character-healthy leaders. I know we are not alone in our desire to see parents raise Godly children. Thousands of you have joined us and I know that thousands more will come alongside us in the future. Because of the broad audience the film has attracted, I now know that we are not alone in our crazy quest to change the world, and it greatly reassures me that God is at work lifting up likeminded believers, all around the globe.

In the final analysis, the film is not so much a documentary about the events of September 11th, 2001, as it is a modern day look at substitutionary atonement. What does it mean to have someone die in your place and what if that person were doing so out of love for you and faithful obedience to God? The essence of the Gospel is wrapped up in Jesus' willing, loving, and compelling trip to the cross, on our behalf. "In My Seat" gently confronts us with a modern day view of just such a love.

Warmest regards,
Steve Scheibner

About Megan Scheibner

Megan was born March 13th 1962 and came home to her adoptive family March 15th. She grew up in York, PA and graduated from York Suburban H.S. in 1980. Four years later, she earned a B.A. in Speech Communications from West Chester University. She uses her degree as she teaches and speaks at conferences and women's ministry functions, as well as in individual and couples counseling.

Megan is the home schooling mother of eight beautiful children, four boys and four girls. She has been married for 28 years to her college sweetheart, Steve Scheibner. Together they have co-authored Parenting Matters, The Nine Practices of the Pro-Active Parent. She is also the author of a series of discipleship books for mothers and several devotional Bible studies. Her latest book is titled "In My Seat," the story of Steve's 9/11 experience, that has captivated millions on YouTube.

Megan and Steve have a strong desire to equip today's parents to raise the next generation of character healthy leaders. In her spare time, she loves to run and play tennis. Megan enjoys writing, cooking, feeding teenagers, reading, and everything pertaining to the Boston Red Sox.

Books by Megan:

In My Seat: A Pilot's Story From Sept.10th-11th.

Grand Slam: A Four Week Devotional Bible Study For Christian Athletes.

Rise and Shine: Recipes and Routines For Your Morning.

Lunch and Literature.

Dinner and Discipleship.

Studies in Character.

The King of Thing and The Kingdom of Thingdom.

You can find these books and more resources at Characterhealth.com

Meet Team Scheibner

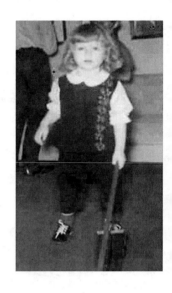

Molly, Emma, and Katie, with their
American Girl Dolls

Megan as an early
Domestic Diva ala 1964

Look at those thighs…
Emma is now married.
My, how time flies!

The Girls and Dolls Reprise

Our last family photo before the year of weddings.

Megan poses with Peter in
Cherryville, PA

Emma serves up a meal as a
young girl. She is now a
professional chef.

Megan as a young girl growing up in York, PA. Remember Izod's?

Our Wedding Day July 7th, 1984

Steve holds our second arrival, Peter (The Film Maker).

Contact Us

Steve and Megan travel extensively facilitating parenting, marriage, men's and women's conferences for churches and other organizations.

Conferences available include:
- Parenting Matters
- Marriage Matters
- Character Matters
- Second Mile Leadership For Men
- The Wise Wife
- The A to Z of a Character Healthy Homeschool
- Woman to Woman: The Mentoring Model and more...

To Speak with Steve or Megan please call:

1-877-577-2736

Or send them an email by clicking the "Contact us" tab at:

Characterhealth.com

Also, follow us on Twitter:
@SteveScheibner
@MeganScheibner